OECD/G20 Base Erosion and Profit Shifting Project

Making Dispute Resolution More Effective - MAP Peer Review Report, United States (Stage 1)

INCLUSIVE FRAMEWORK ON BEPS: ACTION 14

This document, as well as any data and any map included herein, are without prejudice to the status of or sovereignty over any territory, to the delimitation of international frontiers and boundaries and to the name of any territory, city or area.

Please cite this publication as:
OECD (2017), *Making Dispute Resolution More Effective - MAP Peer Review Report, United States (Stage 1): Inclusive Framework on BEPS: Action 14*, OECD/G20 Base Erosion and Profit Shifting Project, OECD Publishing, Paris.
http://dx.doi.org/10.1787/9789264282698-en

ISBN 978-92-64-28268-1 (print)
ISBN 978-92-64-28269-8 (PDF)

Series: OECD/G20 Base Erosion and Profit Shifting Project
ISSN 2313-2604 (print)
ISSN 2313-2612 (online)

The statistical data for Israel are supplied by and under the responsibility of the relevant Israeli authorities. The use of such data by the OECD is without prejudice to the status of the Golan Heights, East Jerusalem and Israeli settlements in the West Bank under the terms of international law.

Photo credits: Cover © ninog-Fotolia.com

Corrigenda to OECD publications may be found on line at: *www.oecd.org/about/publishing/corrigenda.htm*.
© OECD 2017

You can copy, download or print OECD content for your own use, and you can include excerpts from OECD publications, databases and multimedia products in your own documents, presentations, blogs, websites and teaching materials, provided that suitable acknowledgement of OECD as source and copyright owner is given. All requests for public or commercial use and translation rights should be submitted to *rights@oecd.org*. Requests for permission to photocopy portions of this material for public or commercial use shall be addressed directly to the Copyright Clearance Center (CCC) at *info@copyright.com* or the Centre français d'exploitation du droit de copie (CFC) at *contact@cfcopies.com*.

Foreword

The integration of national economies and markets has increased substantially in recent years, putting a strain on the international tax rules, which were designed more than a century ago. Weaknesses in the current rules create opportunities for base erosion and profit shifting (BEPS), requiring bold moves by policy makers to restore confidence in the system and ensure that profits are taxed where economic activities take place and value is created.

Following the release of the report *Addressing Base Erosion and Profit Shifting* in February 2013, OECD and G20 countries adopted a 15-point Action Plan to address BEPS in September 2013. The Action Plan identified 15 actions along three key pillars: introducing coherence in the domestic rules that affect cross-border activities, reinforcing substance requirements in the existing international standards, and improving transparency as well as certainty.

After two years of work, measures in response to the 15 actions were delivered to G20 Leaders in Antalya in November 2015. All the different outputs, including those delivered in an interim form in 2014, were consolidated into a comprehensive package. The BEPS package of measures represents the first substantial renovation of the international tax rules in almost a century. Once the new measures become applicable, it is expected that profits will be reported where the economic activities that generate them are carried out and where value is created. BEPS planning strategies that rely on outdated rules or on poorly co-ordinated domestic measures will be rendered ineffective.

Implementation is now the focus of this work. The BEPS package is designed to be implemented via changes in domestic law and practices, and via treaty provisions. With the negotiation for a multilateral instrument (MLI) having been finalised in 2016 to facilitate the implementation of the treaty related measures, 67 countries signed the MLI on 7 June 2017, paving the way for swift implementation of the treaty related measures. OECD and G20 countries also agreed to continue to work together to ensure a consistent and co-ordinated implementation of the BEPS recommendations and to make the project more inclusive. Globalisation requires that global solutions and a global dialogue be established which go beyond OECD and G20 countries.

A better understanding of how the BEPS recommendations are implemented in practice could reduce misunderstandings and disputes between governments. Greater focus on implementation and tax administration should therefore be mutually beneficial to governments and business. Proposed improvements to data and analysis will help support ongoing evaluation of the quantitative impact of BEPS, as well as evaluating the impact of the countermeasures developed under the BEPS Project.

As a result, the OECD established an Inclusive Framework on BEPS, bringing all interested and committed countries and jurisdictions on an equal footing in the Committee on Fiscal Affairs and all its subsidiary bodies. The Inclusive Framework, which already has more than 100 members, will monitor and peer review the implementation of the minimum standards as well as complete the work on standard setting to address BEPS issues. In addition to BEPS Members, other international organisations and regional tax bodies are involved in the work of the Inclusive Framework, which also consults business and the civil society on its different work streams.

Table of contents

Foreword 3

Table of contents 5

Abbreviations and acronyms 7

Executive summary 9

Introduction 11
Available mechanisms in the United States to resolve tax treaty-related disputes 11
Recent developments in the United States 11
Basis for the peer review process.. 12
Overview of MAP caseload in the United States 13
General outline of the peer review report... 13

Bibliography 15

Part A **Preventing Disputes**... 16

[A.1] Include Article 25(3), first sentence, of the *OECD Model Tax Convention*
in tax treaties 16
[A.2] Provide roll-back of bilateral APAs in appropriate cases... 17

Bibliography 20

Part B **Availability and Access to MAP** 21

[B.1] Include Article 25(1) of the *OECD Model Tax Convention* in tax treaties................... 21
[B.2] Allow submission of MAP requests to the competent authority of either treaty
partner, or, alternatively, introduce a bilateral consultation or notification process 24
[B.3] Provide access to MAP in transfer pricing cases 26
[B.4] Provide access to MAP in relation to the application of anti-abuse provisions............ 27
[B.5] Provide access to MAP in cases of audit settlements 29
[B.6] Provide access to MAP if required information is submitted 30
[B.7] Include Article 25(3), second sentence, of the *OECD Model Tax Convention*
in tax treaties 32
[B.8] Publish clear and comprehensive MAP guidance.. 33
[B.9] Make MAP guidance available and easily accessible and publish MAP profile 36
[B.10] Clarify in MAP guidance that audit settlements do not preclude access to
MAP   37

Part C **Resolution of MAP Cases**.. 41

[C.1] Include Article 25(2), first sentence, of the *OECD Model Tax Convention*
in tax treaties 41
[C.2] Seek to resolve MAP cases within a 24-month average timeframe.............................. 42
[C.3] Provide adequate resources to the MAP function.. 47
[C.4] Ensure staff in charge of MAP has the authority to resolve cases in accordance
with the applicable tax treaty 52

[C.5] Use appropriate performance indicators for the MAP function 54
[C.6] Provide transparency with respect to the position on MAP arbitration 55

***Part D* Implementation of MAP Agreements** 59

[D.1] Implement all MAP agreements 59
[D.2] Implement all MAP agreements on a timely basis 60
[D.3] Include Article 25(2), second sentence, of the *OECD Model Tax Convention* in tax treaties or alternative provisions in Article 9(1) and Article 7(2) 62

Bibliography 64

Summary 65

Annex A **Tax Treaty Network of United States** 69

Annex B **MAP Statistics Pre-2016 Cases** 69

Annex C **MAP Statistics Post-2015 Cases** 76

Figure C.1	United States' MAP inventory	43
Figure C.2	End inventory on 31 December 2016 (963 cases)	44
Figure C.3	Cases resolved during the Reporting Period (185 cases)	44
Figure C.4	Average time (in months)	49

Abbreviations and Acronyms

ACAP	Accelerated Competent Authority Procedure
APA	Advance Pricing Arrangement
APMA	Advance Pricing and Mutual Agreement Program
IRS	Internal Revenue Service
LB&I	Large Business and International Division
MAP	Mutual Agreement Procedure
OECD	Organisation for Economic Co-operation and Development
TAIT	Treaty Assistance and Interpretation Team
USSR	Union of Soviet Socialist Republics

Executive summary

The United States has a relatively large tax treaty network with over 50 tax treaties. It has an established Mutual Agreement Procedure (MAP) program and has extensive experience in resolving MAP cases. It has a very large MAP inventory with a substantial number of new cases submitted each year and more than 900 cases pending on 31 December 2016, of which approximately 75% concern attribution / allocation cases. Overall the United States meets most of the elements of the Action 14 Minimum Standard. Where it has deficiencies, the United States is working to address them.

All of the United States' tax treaties include a provision relating to MAP, which generally follow paragraphs 1 through 3 of Article 25 of the *Model Tax Convention on Income and on Capital 2014* (*OECD Model Tax Convention*, OECD 2015). Its treaty network is largely consistent with the requirements of the Action 14 Minimum Standard, whereby under 11 treaties taxpayers are already allowed to submit a MAP request to the competent authorities of either state in line with the new text of Article 25(1), first sentence, of the *OECD Model Tax Convention* (OECD, 2015), as amended by the final report on Action 14. However, not all treaties are consistent with the requirements of the Action 14 Minimum Standard, as:

- some treaties do not include the full equivalent of 25(2), first sentence, of the *OECD Model Tax Convention* (OECD, 2015), as for example the sentence relating to providing for unilateral relief prior to the referral of the case to the bilateral phase of the MAP is missing;

- one third of its treaties do not include the full equivalent of Article 25(2), second sentence, of the OECD Model Convention (OECD, 2015) (requiring that mutual agreements shall be implemented notwithstanding any time limits in domestic law), or include wording that might obstruct the implementation of MAP agreements by both treaty partners. None of these treaties include the alternative provisions for Article 9(1) and Article 7(2) to set a time limit for making transfer pricing adjustments; and

- one fourth of its treaties do not include the equivalent of Article 25(3), second sentence, of the *OECD Model Tax Convention* (OECD, 2015) allowing competent authorities to consult together for the elimination of double taxation in cases not provided for in their tax treaties.

In order to be fully compliant with all four key areas of an effective dispute resolution mechanism under the Action 14 Minimum Standard, the United States needs to amend and update a certain number of its tax treaties. In this respect, the United States reported that it intends to implement the required elements under this standard in all its tax treaties and that it would conduct any ongoing or future negotiations with current or prospective treaty partners with a view to be compliant with the Action 14 Minimum Standard.

The United States meets the Action 14 Minimum Standard concerning the prevention of disputes. It has extensive experience with bilateral APAs. Its APA program also enables taxpayers to request rollbacks of bilateral APAs.

The United States also meets the requirements regarding the availability and access to MAP under the Action 14 Minimum Standard. It provides access to MAP in all eligible cases. It has in place a notification and consultation process for those situations in which the United States' competent authority considers the objection raised by taxpayers in a MAP request as not justified. It also has in place an internal statutory or administrative dispute settlement/resolution process that is independent from the audit and examination function and that can only be accessed through a request by the taxpayer. Where cases are resolved through that process access to MAP may be limited in the United States. Not all treaty partners, however, were notified of the existence of this process. Furthermore, the United States has extensive and comprehensive guidance on inter alia the availability of MAP and on how the MAP function in the United States is construed and applied in practice.

Furthermore, the United States' competent authority operates fully independently from the audit function of the tax authorities and uses a pragmatic approach to resolve MAP cases in an effective and efficient manner. Its organisation is adequate and the performance indicators used are appropriate to perform the MAP function. The United States therefore meets the requirements under the Action 14 Minimum Standard in relation to the resolution of MAP cases. Concerning the average time needed to resolve MAP cases, the MAP statistics for the year 2016 are as follows:

2016	Opening Inventory on 1/1/2016	Cases started	Cases closed	End inventory on 31/12/2016	Average time to resolve cases (in months)(*)
Attribution/ allocation cases	716	128	145	699	31.61
Other cases	256	48	40	264	28.19
Total	972	176	185	963	30.87

(*) The average time taken for resolving MAP cases for post-2015 cases follows the MAP Statistics Reporting Framework. For computing the average time taken for resolving pre-2016 MAP cases, the United States used as a start date the date when the MAP request was received or notification was given by the other competent authority and as the end date the date of the closing letter to the taxpayer, or, where the case was only initiated with the treaty partner, the date of the closing letter to the other competent authority.

These figures point out that the number of cases the United States resolved is slightly higher than the number of all cases started in 2016, and its MAP inventory as per 31 December 2016 almost remained the same as compared to its inventory as per 1 January 2016. Although the current available resources for the MAP function in the United States are in principle adequate to manage the influx of new MAP cases, a more adequate use of resources available for the competent authority function may be necessary to achieve a net reduction of its MAP inventory. This also because the United States' competent authority did not resolve MAP cases on average within a timeframe of 24 months (which is the pursued average for resolving MAP cases received on or after 1 January 2016), as the average time necessary was 30.87 months, which is comparably similar for attribution/allocation cases and other cases.

Lastly, the United States also meets the Action 14 Minimum Standard as regards the implementation of MAP agreements. The United States monitors implementation and no issues have surfaced throughout the peer review process.

Introduction

Available mechanisms in the United States to resolve tax treaty-related disputes

The United States has entered into 60 tax treaties on income (and/or capital), 58 of which are in force.[1] These 60 treaties apply to 68 jurisdictions.[2] All 60 treaties provide for a mutual agreement procedure for resolving disputes on the interpretation and application of the provisions of the tax treaty. In addition, 4 of these 60 treaties provide for a mandatory and binding arbitration procedure as a final stage to the mutual agreement procedure.[3] In addition, the United States has signed amendments to three existing treaties to incorporate a mandatory and binding arbitration procedure in the MAP article, although these amendments are not yet in force.[4]

Under the tax treaties the United States has entered into, the Secretary of the Treasury, or his delegate, is designated as the competent authority. The competent authority function with respect to the mutual agreement procedure is, pursuant to Delegation Order 4-12 (Rev. 3) of 7 September 2016, delegated to the Commissioner Large Business and International Division ('**LB&I**') of the Internal Revenue Services ('**IRS**').[5] In the United States the competent authority's MAP function is performed by the following teams:[6]

a) *Advance Pricing and Mutual Agreement Program ('APMA')*: cases concerning transfer pricing and profit attribution to permanent establishments. The APMA team also holds responsibility to handle requests for unilateral, bilateral or multilateral APAs; and

b) *Treaty Assistance and Interpretation Team ('TAIT')*: cases concerning all other articles included in the tax treaties of the United States (i.e. residence status, application of the Limitation on Benefits article).[7] The TAIT team also holds responsibility for cases arising under tax treaties that concern estate and gift taxes.

The United States' competent authority currently employs approximately 110 technical persons, of which approximately 85 work in the APMA team. The TAIT team reports to the Director Treaty Administration, who in turn reports to the Director Treaty and Transfer Pricing Operations Practice Area. The APMA team reports to the APMA Director, who, in turn, reports to the Director Treaty and Transfer Pricing Operations Practice Area.

The governance and administration of the mutual agreement procedure in the United States is published in Rev. Proc. 2015-40 ('**MAP guidance**'), which is available at:

https://www.irs.gov/pub/irs-drop/rp-15-40.pdf.

Recent developments in the United States

The United States signed new treaties with Hungary (04-02-2010), Chile (04-02-2010), Poland (13-02-2013) and Vietnam (07-07-2015), and new amendments with Japan (24-01-2013), Luxembourg (20-05-2009), Spain (14-01-2013), and Switzerland (23-09-

2009), but these treaties and amendments are not yet in force. The protocols with Japan, Spain, and Switzerland would incorporate a mandatory and binding arbitration provision to resolve MAP disputes under those treaties.

Rev. Proc. 2015-40, which is the previously mentioned MAP guidance of the United States, constitutes an update and replacement of previous guidance of the MAP process and function, published in Rev. Proc. 2006-54, 2006-2 C.B. 1035. Prior to releasing Rev. Proc. 2015-40, the United States published a draft of the MAP guidance in Rev. Proc. 2013-78, which invited public comments. Based on the public comments received, the IRS and the United States Treasury Department updated the MAP guidance, resulting in Rev. Proc. 2015-40.

Basis for the peer review process

The peer review process entails an evaluation of the United States' implementation of the Action 14 Minimum Standard through an analysis of its legal and administrative framework relating to the mutual agreement procedure, as governed by its tax treaties, domestic legislation and regulations, as well as its MAP programme guidance and the practical application of that framework. The review process performed is desk-based and conducted through specific questionnaires completed by the United States, its peers and taxpayers.

For the purpose of this report, in assessing whether the United States is compliant with the elements of the Action 14 Minimum Standard that relate to a specific treaty provision, the newly negotiated treaties or the treaties as modified by a protocol, as described above, were taken into account, even if it concerned a modification or replacement of an existing treaty currently in force. Furthermore, the treaty analysis also takes into account the treaty with the former USSR because this treaty is still being applied by the United States with respect to nine jurisdictions (see above). As it concerns one tax treaty that is applicable to multiple jurisdictions, this treaty is only counted as one treaty for this purpose. Reference is made to Annex A for the overview of the United States' tax treaties regarding the mutual agreement procedure.

The questionnaires for the peer review process were sent to the United States and the peers on 5 December 2016. While the commitment to the Action 14 Minimum Standard only starts from 1 January 2016, the United States opted to provide information on the period starting as from 1 January 2014 (the '**look back period**') and requested peer input relating to the look back period. In addition to its assessment on the compliance with the Action 14 Minimum Standard, the United States also asked for peer input on best practices.

In total 20 peers provided input: Australia, Belgium, Canada, People's Republic of China, Denmark, France, Germany, India, Ireland, Italy, Japan, Korea, Mexico, the Netherlands, New Zealand, Norway, Spain, Sweden, Switzerland and the United Kingdom. These peers represent 100% of post-2015 MAP cases in the United States' inventory on 31 December 2016. Input was also received from taxpayers. Broadly all peers indicated having good working relationships with the United States with regard to MAP, some of them emphasising the joint effort put forth to successfully resolve disputes.

The United States provided extensive answers in its questionnaire, which was submitted on time. The United States was very responsive in the course of the drafting of the peer review report by responding timely and comprehensively to requests for additional information, and provided further clarity where necessary. In addition, the United States provided the following information:

- MAP profile;[8] and
- MAP statistics[9] according to the MAP Statistics Reporting Framework[10] (see below).

Finally, the United States is an active member of the FTA MAP Forum and currently serves as its chair. It has shown good cooperation during the peer review process. Furthermore, the United States provided detailed peer input and made constructive suggestions on how to improve the process with the concerned assessed jurisdictions. The United States also provided peer input on the best practices for a number of jurisdictions that asked for it.

Overview of MAP caseload in the United States

The analysis of the United States' MAP caseload relates to the period starting on 1 January 2016 (the '**Reporting Period**'). According to the statistics provided by the United States, on 31 December 2016 its MAP inventory was 963 cases, 699 of which concern attribution/allocation cases and 264 other cases. During the Reporting Period 176 cases were initiated and 185 cases were resolved.

General outline of the peer review report

This report includes an evaluation of the United States' implementation of the Action 14 Minimum Standard. The report comprises the following four sections:

- A. Preventing Disputes;
- B. Availability and Access to MAP;
- C. Resolution of MAP cases; and
- D. Implementation of MAP agreements.

Each of these sections is divided into elements of the Action 14 Minimum Standard, as described in the terms of reference to monitor and review the implementing of the BEPS Action 14 Minimum Standard to make dispute resolution mechanisms more effective ("**Terms of Reference**").[11] Apart from analysing the United States' legal framework and its administrative practice, the report also incorporates peer input and responses to such input by the United States. Furthermore, the report depicts the changes adopted and plans shared by the United States to implement elements of the Action 14 Minimum Standard where relevant. The conclusion of each element identifies areas for improvement (if any) and provides for recommendations how the specific area for improvement should be addressed.

The objective of Action 14 Minimum Standard is to make dispute resolution mechanisms more effective and concerns a continuous effort. Therefore, this peer review report includes recommendations that the United States continues to act in accordance with a given element of the Action 14 Minimum Standard, even if there is no area for improvement for this specific element.

Notes

1. Most U.S. income tax treaties are available at: www.treasury.gov/resource-center/tax-policy/treaties/Pages/treaties.aspx (accessed on 10 September 2017).

2. The United States continues to apply the 1973 treaty with the former USSR in respect of Armenia, Azerbaijan, Belarus, Georgia, Kyrgyzstan, Moldova, Tajikistan, Turkmenistan and Uzbekistan.

3. This concerns treaties with Belgium, Canada, France and Germany. See element C.6 of this report for a discussion. Reference is made to Annex A for the overview of the United States' tax treaties that include an arbitration clause.

4. This concerns treaties with Japan, Spain and Switzerland.

5. Available at: www.irs.gov/pub/foia/ig/spder/do_4_12_rev_3.pdf (accessed on 10 September 2017). The delegation order sets out in detail which government department holds competence to perform the competent authority function under the tax treaties the United States entered into. Reference is made to section 2.01 of the United States' MAP guidance as set out in Rev. Proc. 2015-40, which provides an outdated definition of the term *'competent authority'*. Rev. Proc. 2015-40 was issued before the re-organisation of the LB&I in February 2016 and the issuance of Delegation Order 4-12 (Rev. 3). The definition of the term *'competent authority'* will be updated in any successor revenue procedures.

6. See also section 2.01 of the United States' MAP guidance as set out in Rev. Proc. 2015-40.

7. If the case under review concerns the existence of a permanent establishment, both the APMA and the TAIT team can handle such case. Both teams will coordinate and collaborate on such cases as well as on any other case as appropriate.

8. Available at: www.oecd.org/tax/dispute/United-States-Dispute-Resolution-Profile.pdf.

9. The MAP statistics of the United States are included in Annex B and C of this report.

10. MAP Statistics Reporting Framework, in *Peer Review Documents* (OECD 2016): www.oecd.org/tax/beps/beps-action-14-on-more-effective-dispute-resolution-peer-review-documents.pdf (accessed on 22 August 2017).

11. Terms of reference to monitor and review the implementing of the BEPS Action 14 Minimum Standard to make dispute resolution mechanisms more effective in *Peer Review Documents* (OECD, 2016): www.oecd.org/tax/beps/beps-action-14-on-more-effective-dispute-resolution-peer-review-documents.pdf (accessed on 22 August 2017).

Bibliography

OECD (2016), *BEPS Action 14 on More Effective Dispute Resolution Mechanisms, Peer Review Documents*, www.oecd.org/tax/beps/beps-action-14-on-more-effective-dispute-resolution-peer-review-documents.pdf (accessed on 22 August 2017).

Part A

Preventing Disputes

[A.1] Include Article 25(3), first sentence, of the *OECD Model Tax Convention* in tax treaties

> Jurisdictions should ensure that their tax treaties contain a provision which requires the competent authority of their jurisdiction to endeavour to resolve by mutual agreement any difficulties or doubts arising as to the interpretation or application of their tax treaties.

1. Cases may arise concerning the interpretation or the application of tax treaties that do not necessarily relate to individual cases, but are more of a general nature. Inclusion of the first sentence of Article 25(3) of the *OECD Model Tax Convention* (OECD, 2015) in tax treaties invites and authorises competent authorities to solve these cases, which may avoid submission of MAP requests and/or future disputes from arising, and which may reinforce the consistent bilateral application of tax treaties.

Current situation of the United States' tax treaties

2. Out of the United States' 60 tax treaties, 58 contain a provision equivalent to Article 25(3), first sentence, of the *OECD Model Tax Convention* (OECD, 2015) requiring their competent authority to endeavour to resolve by mutual agreement any difficulties or doubts arising as to the interpretation or application of the tax treaty. The remaining 2 treaties that do not include the required provision concern the treaty with the former USSR that is applied with respect to nine jurisdictions and the treaty with Pakistan.

Anticipated modifications

3. For those treaties that do not contain a provision equivalent to Article 25(3), first sentence, of the *OECD Model Tax Convention* (OECD, 2015), the United States indicated that it intends to implement element A.1 for all its existing tax treaties. As one of the two treaties regard the treaty with the former USSR, this treaty can in any case not be modified so as to be compliant with element A.1. For the other treaty, the United States indicated that it would conduct any ongoing negotiations or enter into any future negotiations with a current or prospective treaty partner with a view to be compliant with element A.1.

4. Some peers noted that they are either conducting negotiations with the United States or envisaging such negotiations with a view to be compliant with the relevant elements of the Action 14 Minimum Standard.

Conclusion

	Areas for Improvement	Recommendations
[A.1]	Two out of 60 tax treaties do not contain a provision that is equivalent to Article 25(3), first sentence, of the *OECD Model Tax Convention* (OECD, 2015).	Where treaties do not include the equivalent of Article 25(3), first sentence, of the *OECD Model Tax Convention* (OECD, 2015), the United States should request the inclusion of the required provision via bilateral negotiations. Specifically with respect to the treaty with the former USSR, the United States should, once it enters into negotiations with the jurisdictions for which it applies the treaty, request the inclusion of the required provision. In addition, the United States should maintain its stated intention to include the required provision in all future treaties.

[A.2] Provide roll-back of bilateral APAs in appropriate cases

> Jurisdictions with bilateral advance pricing arrangement ("APA") programmes should provide for the roll-back of APAs in appropriate cases, subject to the applicable time limits (such as statutes of limitation for assessment) where the relevant facts and circumstances in the earlier tax years are the same and subject to the verification of these facts and circumstances on audit.

5. An APA is an arrangement that determines, in advance of controlled transactions, an appropriate set of criteria (e.g. method, comparables and appropriate adjustment thereto, critical assumptions as to future events) for the determination of the transfer pricing for those transactions over a fixed period of time.[1] The methodology to be applied prospectively under a bilateral or multilateral APA may be relevant in determining the treatment of comparable controlled transactions in previous filed years. The "roll-back" of an APA to these previous filed years may be helpful to prevent or resolve potential transfer pricing disputes.

The United States' APA programme

6. The United States has implemented a bilateral APA programme and has run such programme since the 1990s. The IRS established the APMA team in 2012, which brought together its MAP and APA program into a single division. The United States' APA programme is available for transfer pricing issues and for issues where transfer pricing principles may be relevant. This applies both to issues which are ongoing in nature or have already arisen. The United States will consider requests for unilateral, bilateral and multilateral APAs.

7. The United States has issued guidance specifically on APAs in Rev. Proc. 2015-41 ('**APA guidance**').[2] This guidance sets out in detail what APAs are, when and by whom they can be applied for, for what issues APAs can be obtained, how the process for obtaining an APA functions in the United States, what information is to be included in a request for an APA, which government institution is responsible for handling APA

requests, the legal effects of APAs and the circumstances in which APAs may be renewed. The appendix to this guidance further includes instructions and requirements on preparing and filing of an APA request in the United States.

8. With respect to timelines for filing of an APA request, section 3.03 of its APA guidance stipulates that the United States normally expects that such a request is filed early enough that the term of an APA can include at least five prospective tax years (see paragraph 10 below). Specifically regarding bilateral and multilateral APAs, the United States – as set out in section 3.03(2)(b) of its APA guidance – requires that taxpayers file a request no later than 60 days after a corresponding APA request has been filed with the foreign competent authority(ies).[3] If taxpayers do not comply with this requirement, then the first year for which an APA is request is submitted is considered a "roll-back" year (see below). In addition, if taxpayers miss the 60-day deadline by more than one year, the first two or more years for which the request is submitted shall be considered roll-back fiscal years.

9. The United States generally apply APAs to prospective fiscal years, but may apply APAs to previous fiscal years, or roll-back years, after coordinating and collaborating with other offices within the IRS. Typically, the term of application is three to five years, but the United States may, as appropriate, enter into APAs for periods ranging as long as six to ten years, and sometimes longer periods.

Roll-back of bilateral APAs

10. In the United States a roll-back will be provided upon request by taxpayers and subsequently approved by the APMA team. In appropriate circumstances, the APMA team may require that a taxpayer accept a roll-back as a condition of obtaining an APA. When a roll-back is involved, the APMA team will coordinate and collaborate with other offices within the IRS. The term of an APA concluded with a roll-back will include both the roll-back and prospective fiscal years.

11. In section 2.02(4)(c) of its APA guidance the United States has set out its general policy for granting roll-back of APAs. In general, the United States considers APA requests and MAP cases as being interconnected and strives to obtain a substantive and procedural consistency between both processes for the purposes of providing tax certainty to taxpayers and the IRS. Therefore, if a MAP agreement also holds relevance to prospective fiscal years, the United States may encourage taxpayers to file an APA request for these years as well.[4] Vice versa, if an issue covered in an APA holds relevance to previous (closed) fiscal years that have not yet been audited, taxpayers may request for a roll-back of an APA. Section 3.03(2) of the United States' APA guidance includes further information on when years are considered prospective years versus roll-back years. The fiscal years that have not yet concluded and for which an APA is requested, are considered prospective APA years. Fiscal years that have ended when the APA is requested are considered roll-back years. When requesting a coverage of an APA to these roll-back years, taxpayers are required to provide the following information in their APA request:

- A list of the proposed roll-back years;

- A demonstration of the proposed covered method(s) to all proposed roll-back years, thereby using the actual data if available; and

- A waiver of ex parte communication.[5]

12. Specifically with respect to granting roll-back of bilateral APAs, section 5 of its APAs guidance sets out the policy of the United States on such allowance. Application of an APA to roll-back years is possible if the United States would agree to accept such fiscal year to be discussed in a MAP. In section 5.04 it is specified that the APMA team will generally not agree to cover closed fiscal years in an APA, except if such closed fiscal year would be accepted to be discussed under the MAP provision and to the extent the applicable tax treaty allows the MAP agreement to be implemented for the respective fiscal year.

Practical application of roll-back of bilateral APAs

13. Peers generally mentioned that they negotiate and agree bilateral APAs with the United States. Not all peers, however, have experience with roll-back of such bilateral APAs for the years under review or in general. In total 12 peers reported they have experiences with the United States regarding roll-back of bilateral APAs. Their experience point out that roll-back of bilateral APAs is possible in appropriate cases and that the United States is willing to enter into discussions hereon. These peers further reported positive working experiences with the United States in the process of effectively providing for roll-back of APAs. One peer in particular noted that it was confident that roll-back would be provided once an agreement on the APAs would be reached.

14. In practice, for years 2014-2016, the United States indicated that APMA received 107 requests for bilateral APAs with roll-backs (32 in 2014, 38 in 2015 and 37 in 2016), none of which were rejected. As of 31 December 2016, 89 of these requests are still pending.

15. Peers reported that since 1 January 2014 taxpayers have in approximately 20 cases requested for roll-back of their bilateral APAs in which the United States is a signatory party. These peers, however, have not specified in how many cases such roll-back was granted or will be granted.

Anticipated modifications

16. The United States did not indicate that it anticipates any modifications in relation to element A.2.

Conclusion

	Areas for Improvement	Recommendations
[A.2]	-	The United States should continue to provide for roll-back of bilateral APAs in appropriate cases as it has done thus far.

Notes

1. This description of an APA is based on the definition of an APA in the *OECD Transfer Pricing Guidelines for Multinational Enterprises and Tax Administrations 2017* (OECD Transfer Pricing Guidelines, OECD 2017) s for Multinational Enterprises and Tax Administrations.

2. Available at: https://www.irs.gov/pub/irs-drop/rp-15-41.pdf (accessed on 10 September 2017). Further guidance on the United States' APA programme is also available at: https://www.irs.gov/businesses/corporations/apma (accessed on 10 September 2017).

3. A corresponding request is considered a substantive filing with the other competent authority(ies) concerned and not the mere filing of a notice of intent to file such substantive request.

4. Reference is made to section 5.01 of the United States' MAP guidance for a discussion of the possibility to roll-on a MAP agreement to future years by means of an APA.

5. Reference is made to section 1.03 and Exhibit 4 of the appendix to the United States' APA guidance. This section stipulates that the APA request that concerns roll-back years should include a waiver of the taxpayer's right to be present during communications between IRS Appeals and members of the APA team.

Bibliography

OECD (2017), *OECD Transfer Pricing Guidelines for Multinational Enterprises and Tax Administrations 2017*, OECD Publishing, Paris, http://dx.doi.org/10.1787/tpg-2017-en.

OECD (2015), *Model Tax Convention on Income and on Capital 2014 (Full Version)*, OECD Publishing, Paris, http://dx.doi.org/10.1787/9789264239081-en.

Part B

Availability and Access to MAP

[B.1] Include Article 25(1) of the *OECD Model Tax Convention* in tax treaties

> Jurisdictions should ensure that their tax treaties contain a MAP provision which provides that when the taxpayer considers that the actions of one or both of the Contracting Parties result or will result for the taxpayer in taxation not in accordance with the provisions of the tax treaty, the taxpayer, may irrespective of the remedies provided by the domestic law of those Contracting Parties, make a request for MAP assistance, and that the taxpayer can present the request within a period of no less than three years from the first notification of the action resulting in taxation not in accordance with the provisions of the tax treaty.

17. For resolving cases of taxation not in accordance with the provisions of the tax treaty, it is necessary that tax treaties include a provision allowing taxpayers to request a mutual agreement procedure and that this procedure can be requested irrespective of the remedies provided by the domestic law of the treaty partners. In addition, to provide certainty to taxpayers and competent authorities on the availability of the mutual agreement procedure, a minimum period of three years for submission of a MAP request, beginning on the date of the first notification of the action resulting in taxation not in accordance with the provisions of the tax treaty, is the baseline.

Current situation of the United States' tax treaties

Inclusion of Article 25(1), first sentence of the OECD Model Tax Convention

18. Out of the United States' 60 tax treaties, 11 treaties contain a provision equivalent to Article 25(1), first sentence, of the *OECD Model Tax Convention* (OECD, 2015a) as changed by the *Making Dispute Resolution Mechanisms More Effective, Action 14 - 2015 Final Report* (Action 14 final report, OECD 2015b), allowing taxpayers to submit a MAP request to the competent authority of either state when they consider that the actions of one or both of the treaty partners result or will result for the taxpayer in taxation not in accordance with the provisions of the tax treaty and that can be requested irrespective of the remedies provided by domestic law of either state.[1] Further, 42 treaties, including the treaty with the former USSR, incorporate a provision equivalent to Article 25(1), first sentence, of the *OECD Model Tax Convention* (OECD, 2015a) as it read prior to the adoption of that report.

19. The seven remaining tax treaties that do not contain a provision equivalent to Article 25(1), first sentence, of the *OECD Model Tax Convention* (OECD, 2015a), either as changed by the Action 14 final report (OECD, 2015b) or as it read prior to that report can be categorised as follows:

Provision	Number of treaties
A variation to Article 25(1), first sentence, of the *OECD Model Tax Convention* (OECD, 2015a) as it read prior to the adoption of the Action 14 final report (OECD, 2015b), whereby the taxpayer cannot submit a MAP request irrespective of the remedies provided by the domestic laws of the Contracting States.	2[2]
A variation to Article 25(1), first sentence, of the *OECD Model Tax Convention* (OECD, 2015a) as it read prior to the adoption of the Action 14 final report (OECD, 2015b), whereby the taxpayer can only submit a MAP request to the competent authorities of the contracting state of which they are resident and/or citizen.	4
A variation to Article 25(1), first sentence, of the *OECD Model Tax Convention* (OECD, 2015a) as it read prior to the adoption of the Action 14 final report (OECD, 2015b), whereby the taxpayer can only submit a MAP request in cases of double taxation contrary to the provisions of the tax treaty and whereby the taxpayer cannot submit a MAP request irrespective of the remedies provided by the domestic laws of the Contracting States.	1

20. Based on the below clarifications, the 4 treaties that only allow taxpayers to submit a MAP request to their state of residence or citizenship, are for the following reasons considered to be in line with this part of element B.1:

- For one treaty this is explained by the fact that the non-discrimination clause covers U.S. citizens which are residents of the United States for treaty purposes; and

- For three treaties this is explained by the fact that the non-discrimination clause does not cover nationals but "citizens", extended specifically to a resident of the other contracting state.

21. Further to the above, one peer reported that the United States requested taxpayers to submit a MAP request in the United States even though they were resident in the other jurisdiction and while the tax treaty requires taxpayers to submit the request in the state of residence. According to this peer, this requirement is not compliant with the tax treaty and taxpayers may not be aware of it. As such process can delay cases to be effectively discussed in the MAP, this peer suggests deleting such requirement to improve the functioning of the MAP, which was also echoed by other peers. The United States responded that, in transfer pricing cases, its MAP guidance requires the U.S. resident participant in a controlled transaction to file a complete MAP request with the United States' competent authority. The United States also responded that it has largely applied this requirement in a practical manner, recognising the burden it could place upon taxpayers in individual cases. In general, the United States not only believes this requirement is necessary for handling the volume and complexity of the MAP cases it receives, but it also believes the rule gives clear direction to taxpayers about the information necessary to effectively discuss the case and, where the case is subject to

arbitration, helps ensure an earlier "commencement date", which generally is the earliest date on which the information necessary to undertake substantive consideration of a MAP has been received by both competent authorities. However, the United States reported it is considering reviewing its current practice. The view of the United States was adhered to by another peer.

Inclusion of Article 25(1), second sentence of the OECD Model Tax Convention

22.   Section 3.04 of the United States' MAP guidance sets out that taxpayers are encouraged to file a competent authority request when an issue that is eligible under MAP arises, or is likely to arise. It also notes that certain U.S. tax treaties may apply specific time limits for filing MAP requests. To that end, the expiration of time limits in the United States' or in the treaty partner domestic legislation will not prevent the consideration of a MAP request by its competent authority under the conditions that: (i) the specific tax treaty permits the waiver of domestic time limits for implementing MAP agreements; and (ii) the requirements under that specific treaty have been met. The U.S. Model Tax Convention is the baseline text used by the U.S. Treasury Department when it negotiates tax treaties and it does not include a time limit for filing a MAP request.

23.   Out of the United States' 60 tax treaties, 20 contain a provision allowing taxpayers to submit a MAP request within a period of three years from the first notification of the action resulting in taxation not in accordance with the provisions of the particular tax treaty, which wording is equivalent to Article 25(1), second sentence, of the *OECD Model Tax Convention* (OECD, 2015a).

24.   The remaining 40 treaties that do not contain such provision can be categorised as follows:

Filing periods	Number of treaties
Filing period more than three years for a MAP request	4
No filing period for a MAP request	36

25.   In the four treaties identified above the time limit for filing a MAP request is four years (one treaty) or five years (three treaties).

Anticipated modifications

26.   For those treaties that do not contain a provision equivalent to Article 25(1) of the *OECD Model Tax Convention* (OECD, 2015a), either as it read prior to or after adoption of the final report on Action 14, the United States indicated that it intends to implement element B.1 for all its tax treaties. In that regard it specifically indicated that it would conduct any ongoing negotiations or enter into any future negotiations with a current or prospective treaty partner with a view to be compliant with element B.1.

27.   Some peers noted that they are either conducting negotiations with the United States or envisaging such negotiations with a view to be compliant with the relevant elements of the Action 14 Minimum Standard. One peer particularly reported that under its tax treaty with the United States a different timeframe is established for taxpayers to have access to MAP. In this respect, and in order to avoid doubts arising from the interpretation of this particular treaty, it mentioned that the United States' competent authority recently has sent a proposal for a Memorandum of Understanding regarding the

timeframe for access to MAP under the tax treaty. Although this particular tax treaty does not include a time limit for filing a MAP request, in paragraph 1, second sentence of the MAP article and is considered compliant with element B.1, the United States clarified that the first sentence of the MAP article includes a time limitation that the United States seeks to reciprocally interpret in a manner that would ensure greater access to MAP.

Conclusion

	Areas for Improvement	Recommendations
[B.1]	Three out of 60 tax treaties do not contain a provision that is the equivalent of Article 25(1), first sentence of the *OECD Model Tax Convention* OECD (2015a), either as it read prior to the adoption of the Action 14 final report (OECD, 2015b) or as amended by that final report.	Where treaties do not include the equivalent of Article 25(1) of the *OECD Model Tax Convention* OECD (2015a), the United States should request the inclusion of the required provision via bilateral negotiations. This concerns a provision that is equivalent to Article 25(1), first sentence of the *OECD Model Tax Convention* OECD (2015a) either: a) As amended in the Action 14 final report (OECD, 2015b); or b) As it read prior to the adoption of the Action 14 final report (OECD, 2015b). In addition, the United States should maintain its stated intention to include the required provision in all future treaties.

[B.2] Allow submission of MAP requests to the competent authority of either treaty partner, or, alternatively, introduce a bilateral consultation or notification process

> Jurisdictions should ensure that either (i) their tax treaties contain a provision which provides that the taxpayer can make a request for MAP assistance to the competent authority of either Contracting Party, or (ii) where the treaty does not permit a MAP request to be made to either Contracting Party and the competent authority who received the MAP request from the taxpayer does not consider the taxpayer's objection to be justified, the competent authority should implement a bilateral consultation or notification process which allows the other competent authority to provide its views on the case (such consultation shall not be interpreted as consultation as to how to resolve the case).

28. In order to ensure that all competent authorities concerned are aware of MAP requests submitted, for a proper consideration of the request by them and to ensure that taxpayers have effective access to MAP in eligible cases, it is essential that all tax treaties include a provision that either allows taxpayers to submit a MAP request to the competent authority:

  (i) of either treaty partner; or in the absence of such provision;

  (ii) where it is a resident, or to the competent authority of the state of which they are a national if their cases come under the non-discrimination article. In such cases, jurisdictions should have in place a bilateral consultation or notification process where a competent authority considers the objection raised by the taxpayer in a MAP request as being not justified.

Domestic bilateral consultation or notification process in place

29. Out of the United States' 60 tax treaties, 11 contains a provision equivalent to Article 25(1), first sentence, of the *OECD Model Tax Convention* (OECD, 2015a) as changed by the Action 14 final report (OECD, 2015b), allowing taxpayers to submit a MAP request to the competent authority of either treaty partner.

30. For the 11 tax treaties that do not contain a provision equivalent to Article 25(1), first sentence, of the *OECD Model Tax Convention* (OECD, 2015a) as changed by the Action 14 final report (OECD, 2015b), the United States' competent authority does in practice notify and consult its treaty partners when access to MAP is denied or it considers the objection raised in the MAP request not to be justified. Section 7.02 of its MAP guidance states that the United States will, before taking the decision to decline a MAP request, notify and (where appropriate) consult with the other competent authority concerned.

Practical application

31. As from 1 January 2014 the United States reported that in two cases the objection raised in a MAP request was considered as not justified. For these two cases no notification was made. In the first case (a pre-2016 case) this was because that particular treaty does allow the submission of a MAP request in either contracting state. The MAP request in the second case concerned an objection to taxation in the other contracting state as being not in accordance with the tax treaty. The United States reported that it considered this taxation actually to be in accordance with the treaty and therefore judged the objection raised by the taxpayer in its MAP request as not being justified. It, however, did not notify the other competent authority concerned, because it was not aware that notification was also necessary in such a situation.

32. One peer provided input in relation to element B.2 and noted that it would strongly welcome that the United States implements a bilateral consultation or notification process when the United States' competent authority does not consider the taxpayer's objection raised in the MAP request to be justified. This peer noted that under its treaty with the United States it does neither receive such notifications nor was it consulted. Another peer, however, mentioned that such notification was actually provided for where the United States' competent authorities considered the objection raised in a MAP request as being not justified.

Anticipated modifications

33. The United States did not indicate that it anticipates any modifications in relation to element B.2.

Conclusion

	Areas for Improvement	Recommendations
[B.2]	The United States has in place a process to notify and consult the other competent authority in cases its competent authority considered the objection raised in a MAP request as not justified. However, because for the period under review no such cases have occurred during the Review period, it was not possible to assess whether the notification and consultation process is applied in practice.	

[B.3] Provide access to MAP in transfer pricing cases

> Jurisdictions should provide access to MAP in transfer pricing cases.

34. Where two or more tax administrations take different positions on what constitutes arm's length conditions for specific transactions between associated enterprises, economic double taxation may occur. Not granting access to MAP with respect to a treaty partner's transfer pricing adjustment, with a view to eliminating the economic double taxation that may arise from such adjustment, will likely frustrate the main objective of tax treaties. Countries should thus provide access to MAP in transfer pricing cases.

Legal and administrative framework

35. Out of the United States' 60 tax treaties, 40 contain a provision equivalent to Article 9(2) of the *OECD Model Tax Convention* (OECD, 2015a) requiring their state to make a correlative adjustment in case a transfer pricing adjustment is imposed by the other treaty partner. Furthermore, 11 treaties include a provision that is similar to Article 9(2) of the *OECD Model Tax Convention* (OECD, 2015a), but uses additional or different wording.

36. Notwithstanding whether the equivalent of Article 9(2) is included in the United States' tax treaties and irrespective of whether its domestic legislation enables the granting of corresponding adjustments, the United States indicated that it will always provide access to MAP for transfer pricing cases. In section 2.01(2) and (3) of its MAP guidance it is noted that the APMA team within the IRS holds primary responsibility for handling MAP requests relating to transfer pricing.

Practical application

37. The United States indicated that its MAP guidance reflects the view of the United States' competent authority that U.S. tax treaties require it to provide access to MAP consistent with all aspects of the Action 14 Minimum Standard unless the treaty text specifically prohibits such access. If this is not specifically addressed in the tax treaty, the United States' competent authority construes the MAP article to allow taxpayers broad access to MAP.

38. The United States reported that since 1 January 2014 it has not denied access to MAP on the basis that the case concerned a transfer pricing case.

39. Peers indicated not being aware of denial of access to MAP by the United States in transfer pricing cases since 1 January 2014. Also taxpayers reported that the United States has not denied access to MAP in such situation.

Anticipated modifications

40. The United States did not indicate that it anticipates any modifications in relation to element B.3.

Conclusion

	Areas for Improvement	Recommendations
[B.3]	-	As the United States has thus far granted access to the MAP in eligible transfer pricing cases, it should continue granting access for these cases.

[B.4] Provide access to MAP in relation to the application of anti-abuse provisions

> Jurisdictions should provide access to MAP in cases in which there is a disagreement between the taxpayer and the tax authorities making the adjustment as to whether the conditions for the application of a treaty anti-abuse provision have been met or as to whether the application of a domestic law anti-abuse provision is in conflict with the provisions of a treaty.

41. There is no general rule denying access to MAP in cases of perceived abuse. In order to protect taxpayers from arbitrary application of anti-abuse provisions in tax treaties and in order to ensure that competent authorities have a common understanding on such application, it is important that taxpayers have access to MAP if they consider the interpretation and/or application of a treaty anti-abuse provision as being incorrect. Subsequently, to avoid cases in which the application of domestic anti-abuse legislation is in conflict with the provisions of a tax treaty, it is also important that taxpayers have access to MAP in such cases.

Legal and administrative framework

42. None of the United States' 60 tax treaties allows competent authorities to restrict access to MAP for cases when a treaty anti-abuse provision applies or when there is a disagreement between the taxpayer and the tax authorities as to whether the application of a domestic law anti-abuse provision is in conflict with the provisions of a tax treaty. In addition, also the domestic law and/or administrative processes of the United States does not include a provision allowing their competent authority to limit access to the MAP for cases in which there is a disagreement between the taxpayer and the tax authorities as to whether the conditions for the application of a domestic law anti-abuse provision is in conflict with the provisions of a tax treaty.

43. The United States indicated that its MAP guidance reflects the view of the United States' competent authority that U.S. tax treaties require it to provide access to MAP consistent with all aspects of the Action 14 Minimum Standard unless the treaty text specifically prohibits such access. If this is not specifically addressed in the tax treaty, the United States' competent authority construes the MAP article to allow taxpayers broad access to MAP. The MAP guidance of the United States, however, does not include information on whether taxpayers have access to MAP in cases in which there is a disagreement between the taxpayer and the tax authorities as to whether the conditions for the application of a treaty anti-abuse provision have been met, or as to whether the

application of a domestic law anti-abuse provision is in conflict with the provisions of a tax treaty.

Practical application

44. The United States reported that it considers cases relating to the application of a treaty anti-abuse provision and cases concerning the question whether the application of a domestic anti-abuse provision is in conflict with the provision of a tax treaty are covered within the scope of the MAP. Accordingly, it reported that since 1 January 2014 it has not denied access to MAP in such cases.

45. Peers have indicated not being aware of denial of access to MAP by the United States in relation to the application of treaty and/or domestic anti-abuse provisions since 1 January 2014. Also taxpayers reported that the United States has not denied access to MAP in such situations.

46. One peer made a remark in relation to access to MAP with respect to the discretionary granting of treaty benefits under the limitations on benefits ('LOB') article in its tax treaty with the United States. This peer stated its understanding that section 3.06(2)(e) of the United States' MAP guidance determines that treaty benefits, which can be granted on a discretionary basis, are not provided to taxpayers if: (i) no or minimal tax is imposed on the item of income in both countries involved, or (ii) where the request for discretionary granting of treaty benefits is solely based on the fact that the taxpayer is a direct/indirect subsidiary of a public trade company resident in a third country. This peer pointed out that this policy bears the risk that in such cases no access to the MAP will be granted and that this may come into conflict with the requirements under element B.4. The United States responded to this input and stated that the discretionary ability for a competent authority to grant treaty benefits for which a taxpayer is not otherwise entitled does not concern a treaty anti-abuse provision. The United States also observed that section 3.06(2)(e) of its MAP guidance does not operate as an outright prohibition of a favourable discretionary determination in the above-discussed circumstances, but rather states that benefits 'ordinarily' will not be granted in these circumstances. The United States further responded that because it concerns a discretionary decision-power to grant treaty benefits, which are not applicable under the general application of the LOB-article, not granting of benefits in such a situation cannot come into conflict with element B.4. In other words, a taxpayer that requests a discretionary granting of treaty benefits under the relevant LOB-article acknowledges that it does not qualify under the pertinent objective test(s) of that article and thus is not entitled to the particular treaty benefits requested. Consequently, a denial of the discretionary granting of treaty benefits does not result in the denial of any treaty benefits for which the taxpayer would otherwise be entitled. In addition, the United States noted that all questions relating to the interpretation or application of such LOB-article, and disputed by the taxpayer because it believes it is entitled to treaty benefits by meeting the requirements of the LOB-article (absent of a discretionary granting of treaty benefits), are eligible for MAP discussions.

47. The clarification provided by the United States points out that there is no limitation of access to the MAP in cases where the application of an anti-abuse provision in tax treaties is challenged by taxpayers. However, the United States' MAP guidance is not univocally clear on this point.

Anticipated modifications

48. The United States did not indicate that it anticipates any modifications in relation to element B.4.

Conclusion

	Areas for Improvement	Recommendations
[B.4]	-	As the United States thus far has granted access to the MAP in eligible cases concerning whether the conditions for the application of a treaty anti-abuse provision have been met or whether the application of a domestic law anti-abuse provision is in conflict with the provisions of a treaty, it should continue granting access for these cases.

[B.5] Provide access to MAP in cases of audit settlements

> Jurisdictions should not deny access to MAP in cases where there is an audit settlement between tax authorities and taxpayers. If jurisdictions have an administrative or statutory dispute settlement/resolution process independent from the audit and examination functions and that can only be accessed through a request by the taxpayer, jurisdictions may limit access to the MAP with respect to the matters resolved through that process.

49. An audit settlement procedure can be valuable to taxpayers by providing certainty on their tax position. Nevertheless, as double taxation may not be fully eliminated by agreeing on such settlements, taxpayers should have access to the MAP in such cases, unless they were already resolved via an administrative or a statutory disputes settlement/resolution process that functions independent from the audit and examination function and which is only accessible through a request by taxpayers.

Legal and administrative framework

50. Audit settlements are available in the United States. Sections 1.01(5) and 6.01 of its MAP guidance sets out that in case taxpayers enter into such settlement with the IRS, the United States' competent authority will not reject a MAP request on the grounds that taxpayers entered into a settlement agreement with the IRS.[3] However, in sections 1.01(5) and 6.03(2) it is elaborated that where a taxpayer enters into a closing agreement within the IRS examination function, the United States will only endeavour obtaining a correlative adjustment at the level of the treaty partner. It will not undertake any actions that would change the determination of taxable income that is reflected in the audit settlement. Although the United States allows access to the MAP in case of audit settlements, double taxation may not always be eliminated in MAP in such cases.

51. The United States has in place an administrative or statutory dispute settlement or resolution process(es). Within the IRS there is an appeals office, which is responsible for administrative appeals and which procedure can be initiated by taxpayers. This appeals office functions independently from the IRS' audit and examination function and has the authority to resolve disputes based on its assessment of the dispute.[4] The United States' competent authority, which is clarified in section 6.04(1) of its MAP guidance, will deny access to MAP to taxpayers who opt to contest an IRS-initiated adjustment through this

appeals office rather than presenting the case to the competent authority within the time limits set forth in the United States' MAP guidance. The United States' MAP guidance also addresses in section 6.04(4) that if a taxpayer submits a MAP request to the competent authority, the taxpayer retains its right to present its case to the administrative appeals office if the issue is not resolved through the MAP. The United States clarified that these rules are intended to encourage taxpayers to seek relief of double taxation through the MAP before entering into an audit settlement. This to ensure that competent authorities have flexibility to resolve double taxation fully through the MAP process. Element B.10 further discusses this guidance.

Practical application

52. The United States reported that it has since 1 January 2014 not denied access to the MAP for cases where the issue presented by the taxpayer has already been dealt with in an audit settlement between the taxpayer and the IRS. Furthermore, the United States has since 1 January 2014 also not denied access to the MAP for cases where the issue presented by the taxpayer has already been resolved through its administrative/ statutory dispute settlement or resolution process that operates independently from the audit and examination functions.

53. Peers indicated not being aware of denial of access to the MAP by the United States since 1 January 2014 in cases where there was already an audit settlement between the taxpayer and the IRS, or where issues were resolved via an administrative or a statutory dispute or resolution settlement process. Also taxpayers reported that the United States has not denied access to MAP in such situation. One peer, however, noted that, although the United States provides access to MAP, double taxation may not always be resolved in case a taxpayer has entered into an audit settlement with the IRS. This is because the United States' competent authority will in such circumstances only present the case to the other competent authority concerned for correlative relief.

Anticipated modifications

54. The United States did not indicate that it anticipates any modifications in relation to element B.5.

Conclusion

	Areas for Improvement	Recommendations
[B.5]	-	As the United States has thus far granted access to the MAP in eligible cases, even if there was an audit settlement between the tax authority and the taxpayer, it should continue granting access for these cases.

[B.6] Provide access to MAP if required information is submitted

> Jurisdictions should not limit access to MAP based on the argument that insufficient information was provided if the taxpayer has provided the required information based on the rules, guidelines and procedures made available to taxpayers on access to and the use of MAP.

55. To resolve cases where there is taxation not in accordance with the provisions of the tax treaty it is important that competent authorities do not limit access to MAP when taxpayers have complied with the information and documentation requirements as provided in the jurisdiction's guidance relating hereto. Access to MAP will be facilitated when such required information and documentation is made publically available.

Legal framework on access to MAP and information to be submitted

56. The information and documentation that the United States requires taxpayers include in a request for MAP assistance are discussed under element B.8.

57. The United States has specified in section 7.01 of its MAP guidance that it will acknowledge receipt of a MAP request to taxpayers and indicate therein whether the request is complete and is accepted. Under section 7.02 and the appendix of its MAP guidance it is clarified that the United States' competent authority is allowed to deny access to MAP if taxpayers fail to provide all substantive information necessary for a consideration of the MAP request, as specified in sections 3.05 and Appendix of its MAP guidance. The allowance to deny access to MAP for incomplete requests, however, does not imply that access to MAP will be denied if taxpayers did not include in their initial MAP request all information that is required. In such situation, the United States' competent authority will correspond with taxpayers and provide them the opportunity to supplement their MAP request with the additional required information. In this respect, taxpayers are provided a reasonable opportunity to correct or remedy any deficiencies in these MAP requests or in subsequent submissions during the MAP process.

Practical application

58. According to the United States it provides access to MAP in all cases where taxpayers have complied with the information or documentation required by its competent authority and as set out in its MAP guidance. Since 1 January 2014 the United States has not limited access to MAP during the Reporting Period on the grounds that information in the MAP request was not the information or documentation required by its competent authority.

59. Peers indicated not being aware of denial of access to MAP by the United States since 1 January 2014 in situations where taxpayers complied with information and documentation requirements set out in the MAP guidance. Also taxpayers reported that the United States has not denied access to MAP in such situation.

Anticipated modifications

60. The United States did not indicate that it anticipates any modifications in relation to element B.6.

Conclusion

	Areas for Improvement	Recommendations
[B.6]	-	As the United States has thus far not limited access to the MAP in eligible cases when taxpayers have complied with the United States' information and documentation requirements for MAP requests, it should continue this practice.

[B.7] Include Article 25(3), second sentence, of the *OECD Model Tax Convention* in tax treaties

> Jurisdictions should ensure that their tax treaties contain a provision under which competent authorities may consult together for the elimination of double taxation in cases not provided for in their tax treaties.

61. For ensuring that tax treaties operate effectively and in order for competent authorities to be able to respond quickly to unanticipated situations, it is useful that tax treaties include the second sentence of Article 25(3) of the *OECD Model Tax Convention* (OECD, 2015a), enabling them to consult together for the elimination of double taxation in cases not provided for by these treaties.

Current situation of the United States' tax treaties

62. Out of the United States' 60 tax treaties, 14 do not contain a provision equivalent to Article 25(3), second sentence, of the *OECD Model Tax Convention* (OECD, 2015a) allowing their competent authority to consult together for the elimination of double taxation in cases not provided for in their tax treaties.

Anticipated modifications

63. For those treaties that do not contain a provision equivalent to Article 25(3), second sentence, of the *OECD Model Tax Convention* (OECD, 2015a), the United States indicated that it intends to implement element B.7 for all its existing tax treaties. As 1 of these 14 treaties regard the treaty with the former USSR, this treaty can in any case not be modified so as to be compliant with element B.7. For the other 13 treaties, the United States indicated that it would conduct any ongoing negotiations or enter into future negotiations with a current or prospective treaty partner with a view to be compliant with element B.7.

64. Some peers noted that they are either conducting negotiations with the United States or envisaging such negotiations with a view to be compliant with the relevant elements of the Action 14 Minimum Standard.

Conclusion

	Areas for Improvement	Recommendations
[B.7]	14 out of 60 tax treaties do not contain a provision that is equivalent to Article 25(3), second sentence, of the *OECD Model Tax Convention* (OECD, 2015a).	Where treaties do not include the equivalent of Article 25(3), second sentence, of the *OECD Model Tax Convention* (OECD, 2015a), the United States should request the inclusion of the required provision via bilateral negotiations. Specifically with respect to the treaty with the former USSR, the United States should, once it enters into negotiations with the jurisdictions for which it applies the treaty, request the inclusion of the required provision. In addition, the United States should maintain its stated intention to include the required provision in all future treaties.

[B.8] Publish clear and comprehensive MAP guidance

> Jurisdictions should publish clear rules, guidelines and procedures on access to and use of the MAP and include the specific information and documentation that should be submitted in a taxpayer's request for MAP assistance.

65. Information on a jurisdiction's MAP regime facilitates the timely initiation and resolution of MAP cases. Clear rules, guidelines and procedures on access to and use of the MAP are essential for making taxpayers and other stakeholders aware of how a jurisdiction's MAP regime functions. In addition, to ensure that a MAP request is received and will be reviewed by the competent authority in a timely manner, it is important that a jurisdiction's MAP guidance clearly and comprehensively explains how a taxpayer can make a MAP request and what information and documentation should be included in such request.

The United States' MAP guidance

66. As mentioned in the Introduction, the United States' rules, guidelines and procedures relating to the MAP function are included in Rev. Proc. 2015-40. This document sets out in detail the use of the MAP under the tax treaties the United States entered into and also describes the approach of the United States on using arbitration where MAP does not lead to the elimination of double taxation. More specifically, its MAP guidance contains information on:

(a) General outline of the MAP function under tax treaties in general and the availability of MAP under the tax treaties the United States entered into;

(b) Performance of the competent authority function in the United States and contact information of the competent authority or the office in charge of MAP cases;

(c) Scope of application of the MAP process (e.g. for which cases taxpayers can and cannot request competent authority assistance);

(d) Procedures for submission of MAP requests by taxpayers, including the manner and form in which the taxpayer should submit its MAP request, as also the usage of pre-filing procedures;

(e) Relationship with domestic available remedies (both domestic court cases, the internal IRS appeals procedure and the simultaneous appeals procedure) and the APA programme;

(f) How the MAP functions in terms of timing, the role of the competent authorities and the rights and role of taxpayers;

(g) Instances where access to MAP may be denied;

(h) Time limits for filing of a MAP request;

(i) The specific information and documentation that should be included in a MAP request (see also paragraphs 68 and 69 below);

(j) Availability of MAP in relation to the Accelerated Competent Authority Procedure[5] ('**ACAP**'), secondary adjustments and ancillary issues, such as the application of domestic legislation regarding penalties, fines and interest;

(k) The possibility to file a small case MAP request;[6]

(l) Implementation of MAP agreements, including the right for taxpayers to accept or reject these agreements;

(m) Information on availability of arbitration and the functioning of the arbitration procedure under tax treaties;

(n) Filing of protective claims to ensure that domestic law regulations do not constrain the implementation of MAP agreements; and

(o) Consideration of interest and penalties in a MAP.

67. The above-described MAP guidance of the United States includes detailed information on the availability and the use of the MAP and how its competent authority conducts the process in practice. This guidance includes the information that the FTA MAP Forum agreed should be included in a jurisdiction's MAP guidance, which concerns: (i) contact information of the competent authority or the office in charge of MAP cases and (ii) the manner and form in which the taxpayer should submit its MAP request.[7] Although the United States' MAP guidance is comprehensive, one subject is not specifically addressed. This concerns a specification on whether the MAP is available in cases of multilateral disputes and the process how MAP agreements are implemented in terms of steps to be taken and timing of these steps, including any actions to be taken by taxpayers (if any).

Information and documentation to be included in a MAP request

68. The United States' MAP guidance enumerates in section 3.05 in what form a MAP request should be submitted and what information needs to be included in such request. The appendix to this MAP guidance sets out in detail the required information

and documentation for MAP requests, and the order in which it should be presented. In addition, this appendix also contains information and instructions on other administrative matters relating to the submission of a MAP request. Section 1 of the appendix lists the instructions and requirements for all competent authority requests, whereas sections 2 and 3 concern MAP requests filed with the APMA team respectively the TAIT team.

69. To facilitate the review of a MAP request by competent authorities and to have more consistency in the required content of MAP requests, the FTA MAP Forum agreed on guidance that jurisdictions could use in their domestic guidance on what information and documentation taxpayers need to include in a request for MAP assistance.[8] In this respect, the requirements in the United States on what on what information and documentation should be included in a MAP request are checked in the following list:

- ☑ Identity of the taxpayer(s) covered in the MAP request;

- ☑ The basis for the request (the nature of the action giving rise to, or expected to give rise to, taxation not in accordance with the convention);

- ☑ Facts of the case;

- ☑ Analysis of the issue(s) requested to be resolved via MAP;

- ☑ Whether the MAP request was also submitted to the competent authority of the other treaty partner;

- ☐ Whether the MAP request was also submitted to another authority under another instrument that provides for a mechanism to resolve treaty-related disputes;

- ☑ Whether the issue(s) involved were dealt with previously; and

- ☑ A statement confirming that all information and documentation provided in the MAP request is accurate and that the taxpayer will assist the competent authority in its resolution of the issue(s) presented in the MAP request by furnishing any other information or documentation required by the competent authority in a timely manner.

70. With respect to the availability of arbitration, the United States has agreed with Belgium, Canada, France, Germany, Japan, Spain and Switzerland that taxpayers must provide information in accordance with domestic rules of each jurisdiction in a MAP request, as a prerequisite for cases to become eligible for arbitration after the expiration of the specific deadline for the mutual agreement procedure.[9]

71. One peer provided input on element B.8. It considered that the United States' MAP guidance contains helpful information on how it conducts the MAP. This peer used this guidance when conducting MAPs with the United States and considered it to be informative. In addition, taxpayers also indicated that the guidance issued by the United States sets out the information to be included in a MAP request in a clear manner, but suggested that the section dealing with arbitration could provide more guidance on how and when cases are eligible for arbitration.

Anticipated modifications

72. The United States did not indicate that it anticipates any modifications in relation to element B.8.

Conclusion

	Areas for Improvement	Recommendations
[B.8]	MAP guidance is comprehensive and available, but some further clarity could still be provided.	Although not required by the Action 14 Minimum Standard, in order to further improve the level of clarity of its MAP guidance, the United States could consider including information on: ○ Whether MAP is available in cases of multilateral disputes; and ○ The process how MAP agreements are implemented in terms of steps to be taken and timing of these steps, including actions to be taken by taxpayers and the timeframe for giving consent to the MAP agreement reached.

[B.9] Make MAP guidance available and easily accessible and publish MAP profile

> Jurisdictions should take appropriate measures to make rules, guidelines and procedures on access to and use of the MAP available and easily accessible to the public and should publish their jurisdiction MAP profiles on a shared public platform pursuant to the agreed template.

73. The public availability and accessibility of a jurisdiction's MAP guidance increases public awareness on access to and the use of the MAP in that jurisdiction. Publishing MAP profiles on a shared public platform further promotes the transparency and dissemination of the MAP programme.[10]

Rules, guidelines and procedures on access to and use of the MAP

74. As discussed in the Introduction, the MAP guidance of the United States is published and can be found at:

https://www.irs.gov/pub/irs-drop/rp-15-40.pdf

75. As regards its accessibility, it is easily found on the government website of the IRS. For example, a search for 'double taxation' on this website is directed towards the relevant webpage, where the public guidance on MAP can be found. Furthermore, for each tax treaty the United States has entered into a unilateral technical explanation to the tax treaty is provided for.[11]

MAP profile

76. The MAP profile of the United States is published on the website of the OECD.[12] This MAP profile is complete and often with detailed information. This profile includes external links which provide extra information and guidance.

Anticipated modifications

77. The United States did not indicate that it anticipates any modifications in relation to element B.9.

Conclusion

	Areas for Improvement	Recommendations
[B.9]	-	The United States should ensure that future updates of its MAP guidance are made publically available and easily accessible and that its MAP profile, published on the shared public platform, is updated if needed.

[B.10] Clarify in MAP guidance that audit settlements do not preclude access to MAP

> Jurisdictions should clarify in their MAP guidance that audit settlements between tax authorities and taxpayers do not preclude access to MAP. If jurisdictions have an administrative or statutory dispute settlement/resolution process independent from the audit and examination functions and that can only be accessed through a request by the taxpayer, and jurisdictions limit access to the MAP with respect to the matters resolved through that process, jurisdictions should notify their treaty partners of such administrative or statutory processes and should expressly address the effects of those processes with respect to the MAP in their public guidance on such processes and in their public MAP programme guidance.

78. As explained under element B.5 an audit settlement can be valuable to taxpayers by providing certainty to them on their tax position. Nevertheless, as double taxation may not be fully eliminated by agreeing with such settlements, it is important that a jurisdiction's MAP guidance clarifies that in case of audit settlement taxpayers have access to the MAP. In addition, for providing clarity on the relationship between administrative or statutory dispute settlement or resolution processes and the MAP (if any), it is critical that both the public guidance on such processes and the public MAP programme guidance address the effects of those processes, if any. Finally, as the MAP represents a collaborative approach between treaty partners, it is helpful that treaty partners are notified of each other's MAP programme and limitations thereto, particularly in relation to the previous mentioned processes.

MAP and audit settlements in the MAP guidance

79. As previously discussed under element B.5, the United States' MAP guidance includes in section 6.03 an explanation of the relationship between access to the MAP and audit settlements. This guidance clarifies that taxpayers have access to MAP in cases where they entered into an audit settlement with the IRS' examination function, but that the United States will only present the case to the treaty partner for correlative relief in such circumstances.

80. Peers generally indicated not being aware that audit settlements may preclude access to the MAP in the United States. One peer, however, referred to section 6.03(2) of the United States' MAP guidance and pointed out that this policy may, as noted in paragraph 53 under element B.5, jeopardise the elimination of double taxation in cases where the taxpayer entered into a settlement agreement with the IRS.

MAP and other administrative or statutory dispute settlement/resolution processes in available guidance

81. As previously discussed under element B.5, the United States has an internal statutory/administrative dispute settlement/resolution process in place that is independent from the audit and examination function and that can only be accessed through a request by the taxpayer as an alternative to, and in some ways in conjunction with, the MAP process.

82. Section 6.04(1) of its MAP guidance explains that the United States' competent authority will deny access to MAP for those issues in which taxpayers opted to challenge an IRS-initiated adjustment through this process instead of presenting them to the United States' competent authority according to the procedures and deadlines set forth in its MAP guidance. Section 6.04 of its MAP guidance further details the rules that apply when taxpayers opt for an internal administrative appeal with the IRS appeals office and its interrelation with the availability of MAP for those issues settled through that process. In section 6.04(3) it is further specified that the United States' competent authority will require that the MAP request severs, or separates out, issues that are to be submitted for competent authority assistance from those that would remain under review by the IRS appeals office. In other words, only those issues that are not under review by the IRS appeals office can be dealt with in a MAP.

83. Furthermore, the United States has included information on the internal administrative appeal with the IRS appeals office in the IRS Internal Revenue Manual. This manual can be found at: https://www.irs.gov/irm/part8/irm_08-007-003.html#d0e1133. Section 8.7.3.7 of this manual includes specific information on how the administrative appeals interrelate with the mutual agreement procedure under tax treaties the United States entered into.

Notification of treaty partners of existing administrative or statutory dispute settlement/resolution processes

84. The United States reported that all treaty partners were notified of the existence of its statutory/administrative dispute settlement/resolution process and its consequences for MAP, because this process is identified and described in the United States' MAP guidance and MAP profile, both of which are publicly available. All 19 peers that provided input on the United States' compliance with the Action 14 Minimum Standard, however, reported that they were not notified of the existence of such process in the United States. Two peers indicated that they only learned from the existence of this process via the information included in the United States' MAP profile as published on the website of the OECD, whereas one peer indicated that such information is not available in this MAP profile. Furthermore, a fourth peer reported that they only learned of the process due to the fact that the existence of such process was brought to its attention in a specific MAP case.

85. While the United States did not separately notify their treaty partners of the existence of its statutory/administrative dispute settlement/resolution process by means of a formal letter, the United States includes detailed information on this process in its MAP profile, with a reference to its domestic MAP guidance in which the process is outlined in detail. This is considered to be in line with the requirement on element B.10.

Anticipated modifications

86. The United States did not indicate that it anticipates any modifications in relation to element B.10.

Conclusion

	Areas for Improvement	Recommendations
[B.10]	-	-

Notes

1. One treaty allows the submission of a MAP request to the competent authority for either treaty partner for cases concerning the attribution of profits to permanent establishments. For simplicity purposes, this treaty was considered as having the equivalent of Article 25(1), first sentence, of the OECD Model Tax Convention (OECD, 2015a) as it read prior to the adoption of the Action 14 final report (OECD, 2015). In the treaty analysis included in Annex A, this treaty has been qualified with O/E.

2. One of these treaties, however, allows the submission of the MAP request to the competent authorities of either contracting state, but for the rest is not equivalent to Article 25(1), first sentence, of the OECD Model Tax Convention (OECD, 2015a).

3. In the United States taxpayers may sign a so-called Form 870 concerning *Waiver of Restrictions on Assessment and Collection of Deficiency in Tax and Acceptance of Overassessment*. Signing this form by taxpayers, however, does not preclude access to MAP.

4. In addition, the IRS and the United States' competent authority has established a simultaneous appeals procedure by which taxpayers may request that the United States' competent authority aligns with the IRS appeals office before it presents its position on a MAP case to the competent authority of its treaty partner. The process is an optional aspect of the MAP process and its application has to be requested by taxpayers prior to or within 60 days after filing a MAP request. In this simultaneous appeals procedure the United States' competent authority, the IRS appeals office and taxpayers working toward the position of the United States regarding the U.S. initiated adjustment that is eventually presented to the competent authority of its treaty partner. Section 6.04 of the United States' MAP guidance includes detailed rules how this process functions. The outcome of this process is neither binding on the United States' competent authority nor on the IRS appeals office and taxpayers. In addition, the outcome does not limit taxpayers' access to MAP. See in this regard section 6.04(2)(ii) of the United States' MAP guidance.

5. The ACAP concerns the possibility to extend a MAP agreement to future fiscal years for which taxpayers have filed tax returns. Reference is made to section 4.01 of the United States' MAP guidance for information hereon.

6. A small case MAP request can be submitted if the sum of the adjustment, either in the United States or in the other jurisdiction involved, does not exceed the threshold of USD 1 million for individuals or USD 5 million for corporations/partnerships. Such small case MAP request cannot be made for cases concerning: (i) taxpayer-initiated adjustments, (ii) requests for discretionary granting of benefits under the limitation of benefits (LOB) article and (iii) pension plan request filed by persons other than individuals. Reference is made to section 5 of the United States' MAP guidance for an overview.

7. Available at: www.oecd.org/tax/beps/beps-action-14-on-more-effective-dispute-resolution-peer-review-documents.pdf.

8. Ibid.

9. Available at: www.irs.gov/businesses/international-businesses/mandatory-arbitration-with-germany-belgium-and-canada (accessed on 10 September 2017).

10. The shared public platform can be found at: www.oecd.org/ctp/dispute/country-map-profiles.htm.

11. Available at: www.irs.gov/businesses/international-businesses/united-states-income-tax-treaties-a-to-z (accessed on 10 September 2017) and www.treasury.gov/resource-center/tax-policy/treaties/Pages/treaties.aspx (accessed on 10 September 2017).

12. Available at: www.oecd.org/tax/dispute/United-States-Dispute-Resolution-Profile.pdf.

Bibliography

OECD (2016), *BEPS Action 14 on More Effective Dispute Resolution Mechanisms, Peer Review Documents*, www.oecd.org/tax/beps/beps-action-14-on-more-effective-dispute-resolution-peer-review-documents.pdf (accessed on 22 August 2017).

OECD (2015a), *Model Tax Convention on Income and on Capital 2014 (Full Version)*, OECD Publishing, Paris, http://dx.doi.org/10.1787/9789264239081-en

OECD (2015b), *Making Dispute Resolution Mechanisms More Effective, Action 14 - 2015 Final Report*, OECD Publishing, Paris. http://dx.doi.org/10.1787/9789264241633-en

Part C

Resolution of MAP Cases

[C.1] Include Article 25(2), first sentence, of the *OECD Model Tax Convention* in tax treaties

> Jurisdictions should ensure that their tax treaties contain a provision which requires that the competent authority who receives a MAP request from the taxpayer, shall endeavour, if the objection from the taxpayer appears to be justified and the competent authority is not itself able to arrive at a satisfactory solution, to resolve the MAP case by mutual agreement with the competent authority of the other Contracting Party, with a view to the avoidance of taxation which is not in accordance with the tax treaty.

87. It is of critical importance that in addition to allowing taxpayers to request for a MAP, tax treaties also include the first sentence of Article 25(2) of the *OECD Model Tax Convention* (OECD, 2015a), which obliges competent authorities, in situations where the objection raised by taxpayers are considered justified and where cases cannot be unilaterally resolved, to enter into discussions with each other to resolve cases of taxation not in accordance with the provisions of a tax treaty.

Current situation of the United States' tax treaties

88. Out of the United States' 60 tax treaties, 46 contain a provision equivalent to Article 25(2), first sentence, of the *OECD Model Tax Convention* (OECD, 2015a) requiring its competent authority to endeavour – when the objection raised is considered justified and no unilateral solution is possible – to resolve by mutual agreement with the competent authority of the other treaty partner the MAP case with a view to the avoidance of taxation which is not in accordance with the tax treaty.

89. The remaining 14 treaties include a provision requiring the competent authority to which the request was submitted, when the claim made by taxpayers is considered to have merit, to strive to reach agreement with the competent authority of the other contracting state. These 14 treaties, however, do not include the complete text as provided for in Article 25(2), first sentence, of the *OECD Model Tax Convention* (OECD, 2015a), specifically the language regarding the possibility of a unilateral satisfactory solution. It is noted that 1 of these 14 treaties concern the treaty with the former USSR. The United States reported, however, that it considers that the absence of such wording in these treaties does not preclude its competent authority from providing a unilaterally satisfactory solution if possible and that it will provide for such relief where appropriate.

Anticipated modifications

90. For those treaties that do not contain a provision equivalent to Article 25(2), first sentence, of the *OECD Model Tax Convention* (OECD, 2015a), the United States

indicated that it intends to implement element C.1 for all its existing tax treaties. As 1 of these 14 treaties regard the treaty with the former USSR, this treaty can in any case not be modified so as to be compliant with element C.1. For the other treaties the United States indicated that it would conduct any ongoing negotiations or enter into future negotiations with a current or prospective treaty partner with a view to be compliant with element C.1.

91. Some peers noted that they are either conducting negotiations with the United States or envisaging such negotiations with a view to be compliant with the relevant elements of the Action 14 Minimum Standard.

Conclusion

	Areas for Improvement	Recommendations
[C.1]	14 out of 60 tax treaties do not contain a provision that is equivalent to Article 25(2), first sentence, of the *OECD Model Tax Convention* (OECD, 2015a).	Where treaties do not include the equivalent of Article 25(2), first sentence, of the *OECD Model Tax Convention* (OECD, 2015a), the United States should request the inclusion of the required provision via bilateral negotiations. In addition, the United States should maintain its stated intention to include the required provision in all future treaties.

[C.2] Seek to resolve MAP cases within a 24-month average timeframe

> Jurisdictions should seek to resolve MAP cases within an average time frame of 24 months. This time frame applies to both jurisdictions (i.e. the jurisdiction which receives the MAP request from the taxpayer and its treaty partner).

92. As double taxation creates uncertainties and leads to costs for both taxpayers and jurisdictions, and as the resolution of MAP cases may also avoid (potential) similar issues for future years concerning the same taxpayers, it is important that MAP cases are resolved swiftly. A period of 24 months is considered as an appropriate time period to resolve MAP cases on average.

Reporting of MAP statistics

93. The United States annually publishes MAP statistics on the website of the IRS, starting as of 2011.[1] These statistics include: (i) MAP requests received, (ii) MAP cases resolved, (iii) the number of pending cases, as per year end, (iv) average time needed to resolve MAP cases and (v) specifically for MAP cases handled by the APMA team; how cases were resolved (double taxation fully eliminated, partially eliminated, etc.). Statistics relating to MAP are also published on the website of the OECD as of 2007.[2]

94. The FTA MAP Forum has agreed on rules for reporting of MAP statistics ('**MAP Statistics Reporting Framework**') for MAP requests submitted on or after January 1, 2016 ('**post-2015 cases**'). Also, for MAP requests submitted prior to that date ('**pre-2016 cases**'), the FTA MAP Forum agreed to report MAP statistics on the basis of an agreed template. The United States provided their MAP statistics pursuant to the MAP Statistics Reporting Framework within the given deadline, including all cases involving the United States and of which its competent authority was aware. The statistics discussed below

include both post-2015 and pre-2016 cases and the full statistics are attached to this report as Annex B and C respectively and should be considered jointly for an understanding of the MAP caseload of the United States.[3] With respect to post-2015 cases, the United States reported having reached out to all its MAP partners with a view to have their MAP statistics matching. The United States indicated that the reported statistics have been reconciled with its MAP partners except for two that did not respond to its outreach.

Monitoring of MAP statistics

95. The United States uses an internal inventory management system to monitor and manages its MAP caseload with all treaty partners.

Analysis of the United States' MAP caseload

96. The analysis of the United States' MAP caseload relates to the period starting on 1 January 2016 (the '**Reporting Period**'). The following graph shows the evolution of the United States' MAP caseload over the Reporting Period.

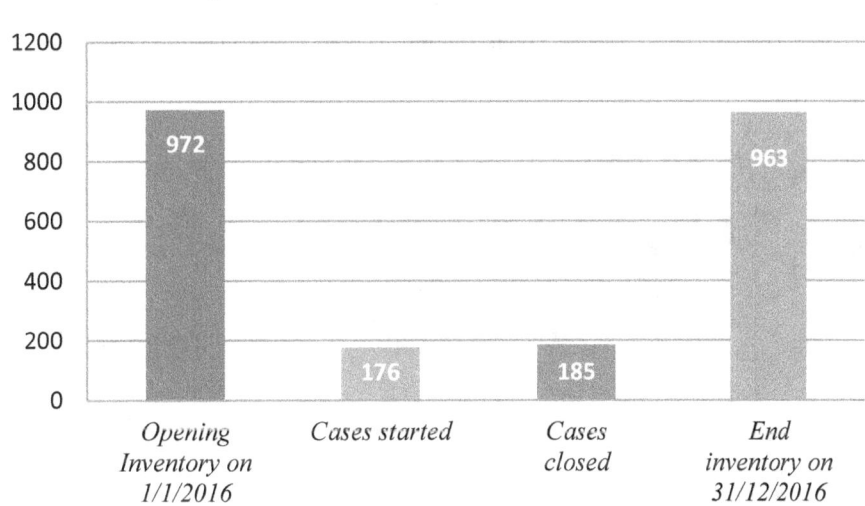

Figure C.1   United States' MAP inventory

97. At the beginning of the Reporting Period the United States had 972 pending MAP cases, of which 716 concerned attribution/allocation cases and 256 other cases.[4] At the end of the Reporting Period, the United States had 963 MAP cases in its inventory, 699 of which are attribution/allocation cases and 264 other cases. The breakdown of the end inventory can be illustrated as follows:

Figure C.2   End inventory on 31 December 2016 (963 cases)

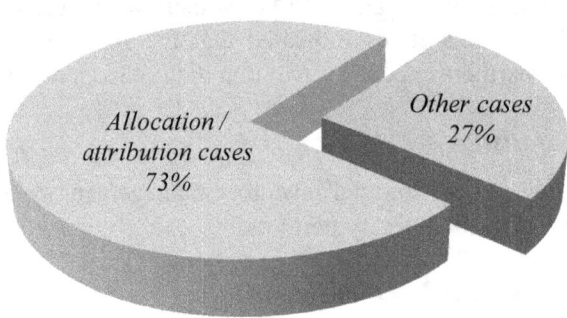

98. During the Reporting Period the United States in total resolved 185 MAP cases, for which the following outcomes were reported:

Figure C.3   Cases resolved during the Reporting Period (185 cases)

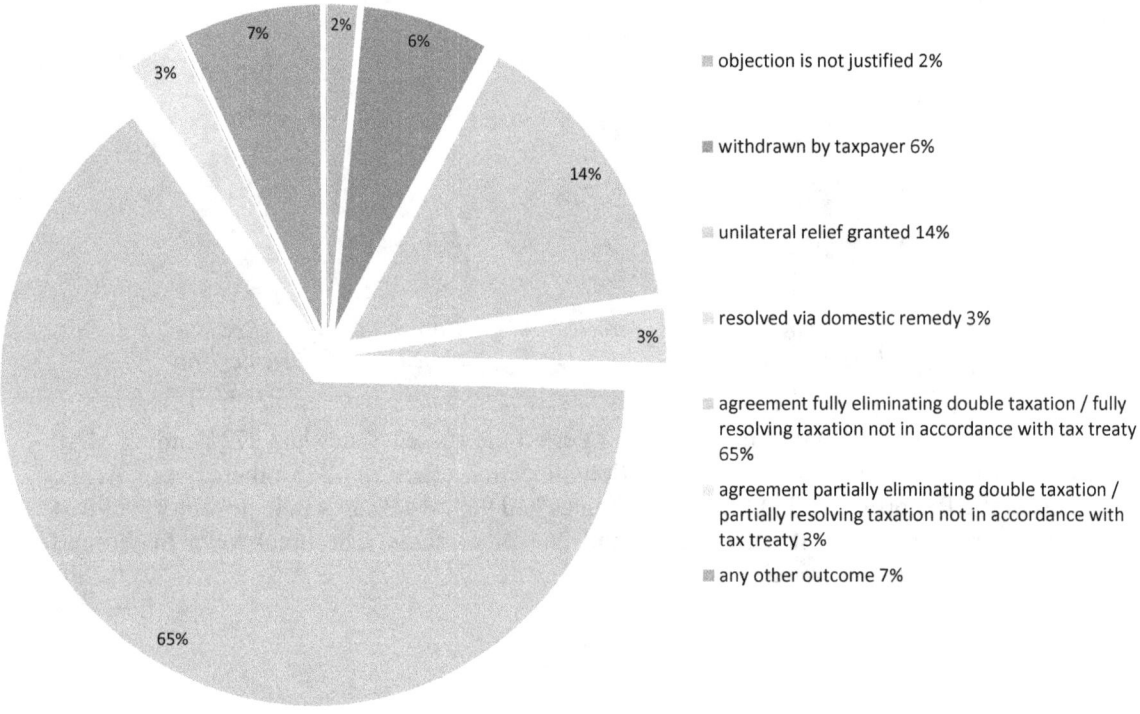

99. This chart points out that during the Reporting Period, 120 out of 185 cases were resolved through an agreement that fully eliminated double taxation or fully resolved taxation not in accordance with the tax treaty.

Managing of the MAP caseload

Pre-2016 cases

100. At the beginning of the Reporting Period, the United States' MAP inventory of pre-2016 consisted of 972 cases, of which were 716 attribution/allocation cases and 256 other cases. At the end of the reporting period the total inventory had decreased to 795 cases, consisting of 574 attribution/allocation cases and 221 other cases. This decrease concerns 18% of the total pre-2016 MAP inventory, which mostly concerned a reduction in attribution/allocation cases.

Post-2015 cases

101. As mentioned in paragraph the United States received 176 MAP requests on or after 1 January 2016, 128 of which concerned attribution/allocation cases and 48 other cases. At the end of the reporting period the total post-2015 inventory had decreased to 168 cases, consisting of 125 attribution/allocation cases and 43 other cases. Conclusively, the United States resolved 8 cases, which reflects 4.54% of the total post-2015 cases.

Average timeframe needed to resolve MAP cases

Pre-2016 cases

102. For pre-2016 cases the United States reported that on average it needed 32.20 months to resolve attribution/allocation cases and 31.50 months to resolve other cases. This resulted in an average time needed of 32.06 months to close pre-2016 cases. For the purpose of computing the average time needed to resolve pre-2016 cases, the United States used:

- *Start date*: the date when the MAP request was received or notification was given by the other competent authority; and

- *End date*: the date of the closing letter to the taxpayer, or, where the case was only initiated with the treaty partner, the date of the closing letter to the other competent authority.

Post-2015 cases

103. As a preliminary remark, it should be noted that the period for assessing post-2015 MAP statistics only comprises 12 months.

104. During the Reporting Period the United States resolved eight cases, three of which concerned an attribution/allocation case and five of which concerned other cases. These resolved cases represent 4.54% of new received post-2015 cases during the Reporting Period. The attribution/allocation case was on average closed within 3.80 months, which led in two cases to an agreement that fully eliminated double taxation/ fully resolving the taxation not in accordance with the provisions of the applicable tax treaty and in one case the request was withdrawn by the taxpayer. The other MAP cases were on average closed within 4.82 months, for which in two cases the outcome was objection not justified, in two cases the taxpayer withdrew its request and in the remaining case there was an agreement that fully eliminated double taxation/ fully resolved the taxation not in accordance with the provisions of the applicable tax treaty.

All cases resolved during Reporting Period

105. The average time needed to resolve MAP cases during the Reporting Period was 30.87 months, which average can be broken down as follows:

	Number of cases	Start date to End date (in months)
Attribution / Allocation cases	145	31.61
Other cases	40	28.19
All cases	**185**	**30.87**

Peer input

106. All peers that provided input to the United States' compliance with the minimum standard report a good working relationship with the competent authority of the United States, which is further discussed under element C.3 below. This concerns both jurisdictions that have a large MAP inventory with the United States and jurisdictions with a relatively modest MAP caseload with the United States. Peers reported that contacts with the competent authority of the United States are easy and that they are solution-oriented. Peers further indicated that cases are generally resolved within a reasonable period, although not all cases are resolved within the targeted 24-month period. Some peers, particularly those with whom the United States has a large MAP inventory, noted that they do not experience any impediments in the timely resolution of MAP cases. These peers in fact appreciated the efforts made by the United States' competent authority to resolve cases within a certain timeframe.

Anticipated modifications

107. As will be mentioned under element C.6, the United States has committed to provide for mandatory binding MAP arbitration in its bilateral tax treaties as a mechanism to provide that treaty-related disputes will be resolved within a specified timeframe.

Conclusion

	Areas for Improvement	Recommendations
[C.2]	The United States submitted timely comprehensive MAP statistics and indicated they have been matched with its MAP partners. The year 2016 was the first year for which MAP statistics were reported under the new MAP Statistics Reporting Framework. These statistics were only recently submitted by most jurisdictions that committed themselves to the implementation of the Action 14 Minimum Standard and some still need to be submitted or confirmed. Given this state of play, it was not yet possible to assess whether the United States' MAP statistics match those of its treaty partners as reported by the latter.	
	Within the context of the state of play outlined above and in relation to the MAP statistics provided by the United States, it resolved during the Reporting Period 4.54% (8 out of 176 cases) of its post-2015 cases in 4.44 months on average.	In that regard, the United States is recommended to seek to resolve the remaining 95.36% of the post-2015 cases pending on 31 December 2016 (168 cases) within a timeframe that results in an average timeframe of 24 months for all post-2015 cases.

[C.3] Provide adequate resources to the MAP function

> Jurisdictions should ensure that adequate resources are provided to the MAP function.

108. Adequate resources, including personnel, funding and training, are necessary to properly perform the competent authority function and to ensure that MAP cases are resolved in a timely, efficient and effective manner.

Description of the United States' competent authority

109. As mentioned in the Introduction of this report, the MAP function in the United States is assigned to the Large Business and International Division ('LB&I') of the Internal Revenue Services ('IRS'). In practice the competent authority function is performed by two teams: APMA and TAIT. The APMA team handles transfer pricing cases, cases concerning the attribution of profits to permanent establishments and APA requests. The TAIT team is responsible for all MAP cases concerning all other articles included in the United States' tax treaties and cases arising under tax treaties that concern estate and gift taxes.

110. The personnel working in the APMA and TAIT teams are generally fully dedicated to dispute resolution. The personnel, however, provides supporting work within the IRS and to the Treasury Department. For example, the TAIT team supports the team that conducts treaty negotiations, as this has a relation with the application and interpretation of tax treaties. Furthermore, both teams may also provide support when drafting internal procedures, such as MAP or APA guidance.

111. The United States' competent authority currently employs approximately 110 technical persons, of which approximately 85 work in the APMA team. According to the United States its extensive MAP experience has ensured that its personnel working in the competent authority have thorough expertise to assist them in resolving tax treaty related disputes. It thereby noted that it consistently looks for opportunities to build internal procedures and mechanisms to support both the APMA and TAIT teams to prevent disputes from arising, to ensure access to MAP where disputes do arise, to timely resolve cases once they are in the MAP and to implement all MAP agreements once reached. Specifically with respect to managing its increasing MAP inventory, the United States' competent authority indicated that it fostered positive treaty relationships and ensured on-going communications and dialogue with its treaty partners.

112. The United States reported that, as a matter of policy, it strives to enter into memoranda of understanding and general competent authority arrangements with treaty partners to address recurring issues that may reduce further potential cases and disputes. The website of the United States' includes an extensive list of these Memoranda of Understanding and competent authority arrangements.[5] The United States, as an example hereof, referred to the recently concluded (October 2016) memorandum of understanding with Mexico.[6] This agreement regards United States' taxpayers that conduct certain business activities in Mexico (maquiladora operations) and ensures that they will not be exposed to double taxation if they enter into a unilateral APA with the Mexican tax authorities on the bases of the terms agreed between the competent authorities of Mexico and the United States. From the perspective of the United States the terms agreed in such unilateral APA are considered at arm's length. These kinds of memoranda of understanding may reduce disputes from arising and also the potential MAP caseload of the United States, by which it can devote the available resources to solving MAP cases.

One peer mentioned in this regard that it has engaged with the United States to address questions on interpreting and applying their tax treaty with a view to agree on a common approach and to reduce future disputes. In practice this has in some instances prevented disputes from arising.

113. The United States has also entered into certain competent authority arrangements specifically relating to the mutual agreement procedure. Two such arrangements are with the Netherlands[7] and the United Kingdom.[8] These arrangements set out certain principles and practices to be followed in presenting and discussing MAP cases. The United States expressed its willingness to pursue such common understandings on best practices with other treaty partners in order to continuously improve the MAP process.

Monitoring mechanism

114. The United States indicated that it constantly assesses workloads, the extent to which additional resources are needed in its MAP function, and its ability to request increased resources based on available budget or reallocate resources across the division.

115. In terms of funding of its competent authority, the United States reported that there has been generally sufficient budget available for travelling and conducting face-to-face meetings.

116. Regarding the monitoring and matching of MAP caseloads with treaty partners, section 12.03 of the United States' MAP guidance notes that its competent authority is not responsible for informing the other competent authority concerned on the receipt of a MAP request. One peer provided input hereon and noted that the United States' competent authority does not inform them of MAP requests submitted, which according to this peer should be the case with a view to having matching MAP caseloads amongst jurisdictions. Another peer reported that it jointly works with the United States' competent authority to align their MAP caseload and the status of MAP requests submitted so as to avoid mismatches between the competent authorities. In a response, the United States reported that it uses an internal inventory management system to monitor and manage its MAP caseload with all treaty partners. The United States reported that it welcomes discussions with treaty partners on how best to share information and update another to most effectively manage respective bilateral MAP caseloads. The United States further reported that it is also beginning to implement procedures to confirm dates relevant to the MAP Statistics Reporting Framework, for example by including its understanding of the MAP start date in notification and acknowledgment letters.

Practical application

MAP statistics

117. As discussed under element C.2, the United States has not resolved its MAP cases during the Reporting Period within the pursued 24-month average. This both concerns attribution/allocation cases and can be illustrated by the following graph:

Figure C.4   Average time (in months)

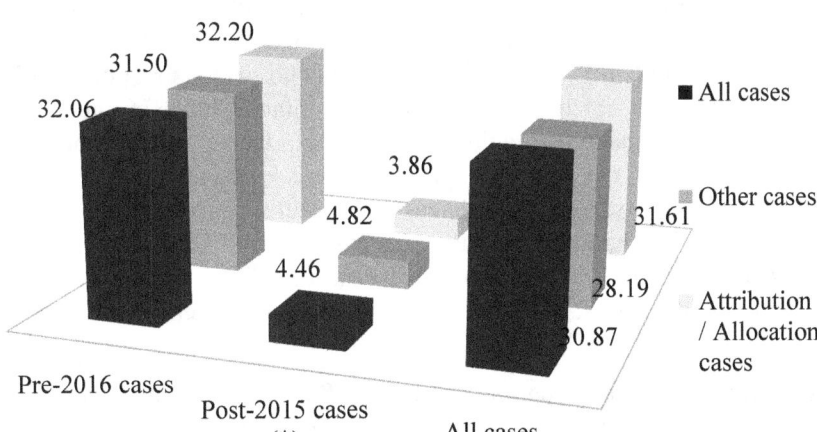

(*) Note that post-2015 cases only concern cases started and closed during 2016.

118. Based on these figures, it follows that on average it took the United States 30.87 months to resolve MAP cases. This figure indicates that additional resources specifically dedicated to these cases may be necessary to accelerate their resolution.

119. The United States reported that there are a variety of reasons why cases were on average not resolved within the 24-month timeframe. It indicated that although resources for the competent authority function might partly explain the overstep of the 24-month average, lengthy resolution of cases are commonly attributable to other reasons, such as delays in correspondence (e.g. sending and receiving position papers), communication difficulties, fundamental differences with treaty partners on points of law or their application to facts, or difficulties in reaching a principled resolution with certain treaty partners.

Peer input

120. As mentioned under element C.2, all peers that provided input report a good working relationship with the competent authority of the United States and that it is an important MAP partner to their jurisdictions. This concerns both peers that have a large MAP inventory with the United States and peers with which there is a relatively modest MAP caseload with the United States. Furthermore, all peers indicated that the contacts with the United States' competent authority are easy and frequent. Methods of communication generally used are mail, e-mail, fax and telephone. One peer particularly noted that the United States' competent authority is very responsive to communication, that there is a constructive and positive cooperation to resolve MAP cases and that it is willing to discuss and conduct negotiations via teleconferencing.

121. With respect to contacting the United States' competent authority peers generally reported that it is considered easily accessible and no problems were reported as regards contacting them. For example, one peer noted that it enjoyed a cooperative and

professional relationship with the United States' competent authority to settle MAP cases, whereby technology and personnel is exchanged between the two states. In addition, this peer reported that there is open communication between their competent authorities, whereby they are aware which persons to contact. Another peer noted that the organisational structure of the United States' competent authority has been explained to them and is considered as a clear division of competence by subject areas. This peer also noted that it is easy to identify the contact details of the persons responsible for a MAP case. In this regard it is noted that the relevant contact details of the United States' competent authority are made available in its MAP guidance. Apart from these positive experiences, one peer noted that it experienced miscommunication with the United States' competent authority, as the peer's competent authority was not promptly notified of changes in the team handling MAP cases with them. Another peer noted that it experienced some difficulties in obtaining a response to official letters sent by them, but it was not further specified what difficulties it concerned and whether and how these were resolved.

122. Other peers, however, reported that United States' policy and practices regarding the timely resolution of MAPs can be improved. For example, one peer noted that in some cases the United States' competent authority sent questionnaires to obtain information, which information could also be obtained under United States' domestic legislation at the level of the taxpayer. Doing so would in this peer's view speed up proceedings. The United States responded that its competent authority considers whether information is available through internal channels before sending questions to its treaty partners. However, when the taxpayer is resident in the other jurisdiction and has not been under examination in the United States, it is unlikely that the United States would have facts and circumstances information relevant to, for example, a residency tie-breaker determination. In these types of cases, the United States agrees that it is more efficient to obtain the information from the taxpayer directly. But if a MAP is initiated by the other competent authority, it is this competent authority that has the primary contact with the taxpayer. Moreover, the United States' competent authority might not have contact details of this taxpayer and there might also be a language barrier in obtaining this information directly from this taxpayer.

123. Another peer reported that the communication process and resolving of MAP cases with the United States may be slowed down due to the confidentiality requirements in place in the United States, which requires that taxpayer identification data can only be exchanged by mail or fax. This peer therefore suggested that to be able to resolve cases more quickly, documents including confidential information are also to be send via encrypted e-mails. From input by other peers it follows that such secured exchange of documents is actually used and facilitates efficient communication between the competent authorities. In this respect, one peer in particular noted that it has agreed with the United States' competent authority on a data exchange set, allowing for quick and secure electronic communications. In addition, another peer mentioned that in some cases it experienced delays in receiving a communication from the United States' competent authority that a MAP case was submitted. This peer therefore suggested enhancing the response and communication time to prevent delays in solving MAP cases within the average of 24-months.

124. Last, a peer mentioned that the United States' competent authority requires legal persons to submit a MAP request in the state where they are incorporated, whereas the treaty in force clearly requires such submission in the state of residence and which requirement may delay the time to resolve the case. The United States indicated that in

transfer pricing cases its MAP guidance requires the associated enterprise resident in the United States, and party to the controlled transaction, to file a complete MAP request with the United States' competent authority. The United States also indicated that it has largely applied this requirement in a practical manner, recognising the burden it could place on taxpayers in individual cases. In general, the United States not only believes this requirement is necessary for handling the volume and complexity of the MAP cases it receives, but also believes the rule gives clear direction to taxpayers about the information necessary to effectively discuss the case. Furthermore, where the relevant tax treaty includes an arbitration provision, the United States has agreed with its treaty partners that taxpayers must – as a prerequisite for cases to become eligible for arbitration after the expiration of the specific deadline for the mutual agreement procedure – provide information in their MAP request that is required by the respective domestic rules of each jurisdiction.

125. On the material side of handling MAP cases, all peers reported that the United States is cooperative, constructive and solution-oriented and has the intent to resolve MAP cases in a timely, effective and principled manner. One peer particularly noted that a substantial amount of disputes have been resolved in 2016 and that both competent authorities showed a high degree of understanding each other's views on the technical issues of the cases concerned. Furthermore, another peer noted that staff in charge of MAP in the United States is well-trained to handle MAP cases. A third peer noted that the United States' competent authority takes a pragmatic approach when an audit by the IRS results in multiple exposures and whereby the covered transactions with some jurisdictions concern only small amounts. Some peers, however, noted that although the United States uses strict requirements on the content of MAP respectively APA requests, its competent authority is flexible and cooperative once cases are in the MAP and negotiations have started.

126. The United States mentioned that its competent authority schedules on regular occasions face-to-face meetings with other competent authorities for settling disputes, whereby frequency of these meetings is dependent on the size and nature of the MAP caseload with the relevant treaty partner.[9] Most peers reported to hold once or twice a year such face-to-face meetings. For all treaty partners, the United States' competent authority meets with its counterparts as needed to ensure that cases progress efficiently.

127. Peers generally reported no items for improvement regarding providing adequate resources for the MAP function. Some peers specifically mentioned that they consider that in the United States there are sufficient resources available to conduct the MAP function. Two other peers also made suggestions for improving the functioning of the United States' competent authority and speeding up resolution of cases, namely: (i) to make more use of video conferencing for discussing cases and (ii) that personnel could be more pro-active in exploring ways to resolve cases prior to face-to-face meetings. Another peer, with whom the United States entered into the previous discussed administrative agreement, mentioned that they strive at bi-annually conducting face-to-face meetings, but not always in succeeding doing so. To enhance communication, this peer suggested making more frequent use of conference calls or videoconferencing, or arranging alternative venues for meetings, for example in Paris during the course of OECD meetings. Finally, one peer also noted that in its view the internal processes in the United States for management oversight/sign-offs of competent authority decisions seem to be unduly extensive. According this peer these processes can be improved in the United States. Another suggestion made by this peer is that the United States' competent

authority could make MAP proceedings more efficient by sharing their reports on the case.

Anticipated modifications

128.   The United States indicated it is exploring and implementing greater use of electronic communications to make communications with treaty partners more efficient, while ensuring applicable data security requirements are met.

Conclusion

	Areas for Improvement	Recommendations
[C.3]	As the United States resolved MAP cases in 30.87 months on average, there may be a risk that post-2015 cases are not resolved within the average of 24 months, which is the pursued average for resolving MAP cases received on or after 1 January 2016 and which might indicate that the available resources in the United States' competent authority are not adequately used.	The United States should ensure that the resources available for the competent authority function are adequately used in order to resolve MAP cases in a timely, efficient and effective manner.

[C.4]   Ensure staff in charge of MAP has the authority to resolve cases in accordance with the applicable tax treaty

> Jurisdictions should ensure that the staff in charge of MAP processes have the authority to resolve MAP cases in accordance with the terms of the applicable tax treaty, in particular without being dependent on the approval or the direction of the tax administration personnel who made the adjustments at issue or being influenced by considerations of the policy that the jurisdictions would like to see reflected in future amendments to the treaty.

129.   Ensuring that staff in charge of MAP can and will resolve cases, absent of any approval/direction by the tax administration personnel directly involved in the adjustment at issue and absent of any policy considerations, contributes to a principled and consistent approach to MAP cases.

Functioning of staff in charge of MAP

130.   The United States reported that staff in charge of MAP holds the obligation to administer and apply tax legislation in a fair and equitable manner, thereby protecting taxpayers' rights and also to treat taxpayers with honesty, integrity and respect. For each case that is handled through the MAP the staff in charge of MAP are obliged to consider and take into account the relevant facts of the case under review, economic analyses, treaty provisions and additional applicable laws for determining how each individual case can be resolved in a principled manner. The United States reported that in the resolution of MAP cases, the staff in charge of MAP must cooperate with the IRS examination department for securing the necessary extensions of the United States' domestic statute of limitations for the period a MAP case is pending. Furthermore, the staff in charge of MAP generally also might consult with the IRS examination department for verifying or gathering the necessary facts for the case under review.[10] In addition, staff in charge of MAP is required to consult with the IRS Office of Associate Chief Counsel International

on certain interpretation matters for ensuring consistency and quality with the tax policy of the United States.

131. With respect to conducting the MAP process and entering into MAP agreements, staff in charge of MAP in the United States is subject to managerial and executive review. Rules relating hereto are set out in IRS Delegation Order 4-12 (Rev.3), which is available on the website of the IRS. In this order it is detailed that the United States' competent authority is allowed to enter into competent authority agreements under tax treaties entered into by the United States. In that regard, the competent authority function in the United States operates fully independent and has the authority to resolve MAP cases. There is neither a (formal) system in place to ask approval for any MAP agreements other than within the competent authority nor a process for negotiating MAP agreements that would be influenced by policy considerations.

132. In the United States, personnel conducting MAP negotiations have the authority to enter into tentative agreements, which are subject to executive approval within the United States' competent authority.

Practical application

133. Peers generally reported no impediments by the United States to properly perform its MAP function, absent from approval or the direction of the tax administration personnel who made the adjustments at issue or being influenced by considerations of the policy. One peer specifically mentioned that they are not aware of any facts indicating that the MAP agreements negotiated by staff in charge of the MAP in the United States are dependent on the approval of the tax authorities outside the office of the United States' competent authority.

134. However, another peer reported experiences that tentative agreements reached between the competent authorities do not always result in a final MAP agreement due to the fact that the tentative agreement is internally challenged in the United States (i.e. due to the fact that the team assigned to the case was changed). This peer therefore suggested that tentative MAP agreements could only be challenged by the head of the United States' competent authority. The United States acknowledged some past confusion on this issue and clarified that, per its current protocols, tentative MAP agreements are internally reviewed and confirmed. They are only subject to challenge by the United States' competent authority and by the director of the applicable office delegated such responsibilities on behalf of the United States' competent authority.

Anticipated modifications

135. The United States did not indicate that it anticipates any modifications in relation to element C.4.

Conclusion

	Areas for Improvement	Recommendations
[C.4]	-	As it has done thus far, the United States should continue to ensure that its competent authority has the authority, and uses that authority in practice, to resolve MAP cases without being dependent on approval or direction from the tax administration personnel directly involved in the adjustments at issue.

[C.5] Use appropriate performance indicators for the MAP function

> Jurisdictions should not use performance indicators for their competent authority functions and staff in charge of MAP processes based on the amount of sustained audit adjustments or maintaining tax revenue.

136. For ensuring that each case is considered on its individual merits and will be resolved in a principled and consistent manner, it is essential that any performance indicators for the competent authority function and the staff in charge of MAP processes are appropriate and not based on the amount of sustained audit adjustments or aim at maintaining a certain amount of tax revenue.

Performance indicators used by the United States

137. The United States does not set targets for the staff in charge of MAP in terms of amounts of sustained audit adjustments or tax revenue maintained. In addition, the performance of the staff in charge of MAP is also not based on the amount of sustained audit adjustments or the maintenance of tax revenue, or the specific results of MAP discussions. In fact, United States' domestic legislation prohibits using quantitative criteria for evaluating the performance of staff in charge of MAP, such as number of cases closed or amount of the tax assessed, or production quotas goals.[11] In general, and in line with the remarks made under element C.3, personnel working in the United States' competent authority are evaluated on critical job elements for their position and whether, consistent with the person's official responsibilities, he or she administers the tax laws fairly and equitably, protects taxpayers' rights, and treats taxpayers ethically with honesty, integrity, and respect. More specifically, personnel in charge of MAP processes are given annual performance appraisals and mid-year progress reports. The United States thereby evaluates the performance of the staff in charge of MAP through using the following qualitative criteria:

a) Workplace interaction and environment;

b) Workgroup involvement;

c) Issue identification and resolution;

d) Technical knowledge;

e) Verbal communication/listening, written communication and interaction;

f) Accuracy of the work;

g) Research and analysis;

h) Security, privacy, disclosure and administration;

i) Planning and scheduling; and

j) Workload management and time utilisation.

138. The Action 14 final report (OECD, 2015b) includes examples for performance indicators that are considered appropriate. These are:

- Number of MAP cases resolved;

- Consistency (i.e. a treaty should be applied in a principled and consistent manner to MAP cases involving the same facts and similarly-situated taxpayers); and

- Time taken to resolve a MAP case (recognising that the time taken to resolve a MAP case may vary according to its complexity and that matters not under the control of a competent authority may have a significant impact on the time needed to resolve a case).

139. Other than consistency, which aligns with the obligation of IRS personnel to administer the tax laws fairly and equitably, the United States indicated that it does not use any of these performance indicators to evaluate its staff in charge of MAP processes.

Practical application

140. Peers generally provided no specific input relating to this element of the minimum standard. One peer noted that it is not aware of the use of performance indicators in the United States that are based on the amount of sustained audit adjustments or maintaining a certain amount of tax revenue. More generally, as discussed under element C.3, all peers reported that the United States is cooperative, constructive and solution-oriented and has the intent to resolve MAP cases in a timely, effective and principled manner.

Anticipated modifications

141. The United States did not indicate that it anticipates any modifications in relation to element C.5.

Conclusion

	Areas for Improvement	Recommendations
[C.5]	-	As it has done thus far, the United States should continue to use appropriate performance indicators.

[C.6] Provide transparency with respect to the position on MAP arbitration

> Jurisdictions should provide transparency with respect to their positions on MAP arbitration.

142. The inclusion of an arbitration provision in tax treaties may help ensure that MAP cases are resolved within a certain timeframe, which provides certainty to both taxpayers and competent authorities. In order to have full clarity on whether arbitration as a final stage in the MAP process can and will be available in jurisdictions it is important that jurisdictions are transparent on their position on MAP arbitration.

Position on MAP arbitration

143. Under the domestic law of the United States there are no limitations for including MAP arbitration in its tax treaties. Inclusion of MAP arbitration is part of its tax treaty policy and the U.S. Model Tax Convention includes a mandatory and binding arbitration procedure as a final stage in the MAP process, which provides for last-best-offer type of arbitration (also known as baseball arbitration). In section 10 of its MAP guidance the United States has set out the basic rules and issues relating to conducting the arbitration procedure.

Practical application

144. Up to date, the United States has incorporated an arbitration provision in 12 tax treaties as a final stage to the MAP. These arbitration provisions can be classified as follows:

- *Mandatory and binding arbitration*: treaties with Belgium, Canada, France, Germany, Japan, Spain and Switzerland; and

- *Voluntary and binding arbitration*: Ireland, Italy, Kazakhstan, Mexico and the Netherlands.

145. The arbitration provisions under the treaties with Ireland, Italy, Kazakhstan, Mexico and the Netherlands are not yet effective, as these only take effect upon the exchange of notes between the contracting states, which so far have not been exchanged. Furthermore, the protocols under the treaty with Japan, Spain and Switzerland that include the arbitration provision have not been ratified, by which these provisions have not yet entered into force.

146. With respect to the above-mentioned mandatory and binding arbitration provisions, the United States has entered into protocols, memoranda of understanding and competent authority arrangements to detail the rules to be applied during the arbitration procedure.[12] Such rules are also agreed on under the treaties with Mexico and the Netherlands.

147. One peer provided input on this element of the Action 14 Minimum Standard. It considered the last-best-offer type of arbitration under its treaty with the United States as working well, since it leads to more reasonable positions taken by their competent authorities, which also contributed that disputes can be resolved without needing arbitration.

Anticipated modifications

148. The United States did not indicate that it anticipates any modifications in relation to element C.6.

Conclusion

	Areas for Improvement	Recommendations
[C.6]	-	-

Notes

1. Available at: www.irs.gov/businesses/corporations/annual-competent-authority-statistics (accessed on 10 September 2017). These statistics are up to fiscal year 2015.

2. Available at: www.oecd.org/tax/dispute/mutual-agreement-procedure-statistics.htm. These statistics are up to fiscal year 2015.

3. For post-2015 cases, if the number of MAP cases in the United States' inventory at the beginning of the Reporting Period plus the number of MAP cases started during the Reporting Period was more than five, United States' reports its MAP caseload on a jurisdiction-by-jurisdiction basis. This rule applies for each type of cases (attribution / allocation cases and other cases).

4. The United States reported that for pre-2016 and post-2015 cases it follows the MAP Statistics Reporting Framework for determining whether a case is considered an attribution/allocation case. Annex D of the MAP Statistics Reporting Framework defines such case as: "*a MAP case where the taxpayer's MAP request relates to (i) the attribution of profits to a permanent establishment (see e.g. Article 7 of the OECD Model Tax Convention (OECD, 2015a)); or (ii) the determination of profits between associated enterprises (see e.g. Article 9 of the OECD Model Tax Convention (OECD, 2015a)), which is also known as a transfer pricing MAP case*".

5. Available at: www.irs.gov/individuals/international-taxpayers/competent-authority-agreements (accessed on 10 September 2017). The content of these memoranda and agreements, as also their public availability, will be further discussed under element B.P 3.

6. Available at: www.irs.gov/uac/newsroom/irs-announces-position-on-unilateral-apa-applications-involving-maquiladoras (accesse on 10 September 2017). Maquiladoras generally operate in Mexico as contract manufacturers of foreign multinationals.

7. See Administrative Arrangements for the Implementation of the Mutual Agreement Procedure (Article 29) of the Convention Between the Kingdom of the Netherlands and the United States of America for the Avoidance of Double Taxation and the Prevention of Fiscal Evasion with Respect to Taxes on Income and Capital Gains (Signed on December 18, 1992, as Amended by Protocols). Available at: www.irs.gov/pub/irs-news/ir-03-116.pdf (accessed on 10 September 2017).

8. See Administrative Arrangements for the Implementation of the Mutual Agreement Procedure (Article 25) of the Convention Between the Government of the United Kingdom of Great Britain and Northern Ireland and the Government of the United States of America for the Avoidance of Double Taxation and the Prevention of Fiscal Evasion with Respect to Taxes on Income and Capital Gains (Signed on December 31, 1975, as Amended by Protocols). Available at: www.irs.gov/pub/irs-news/ir-00-79.pdf (accessed on 10 September 2017).

9. See in this respect also section 2.06 of the MAP guidance of the United States, which stipulates that its competent authority schedules face-to-face meetings with the competent authorities of its treaty partners.

10. See section 4.60.2.4 of the Internal Revenue Manual, which sets out the role of the IRS in the preparation of a report to determine the position of the United States' competent authority in the MAP. This manual is available at: www.irs.gov/irm/part4/irm_04-060-002.html (accessed on 10 September 2017).

11. The United States refers to such criteria as *Records of Tax Enforcement Results (ROTER)*.

12. Available at: www.irs.gov/businesses/international-businesses/mandatory-tax-treaty-arbitration (accessed on 10 September 2017).

Bibliography

OECD (2016), *BEPS Action 14 on More Effective Dispute Resolution Mechanisms, Peer Review Documents*, www.oecd.org/tax/beps/beps-action-14-on-more-effective-dispute-resolution-peer-review-documents.pdf (accessed on 22 August 2017).

OECD (2015a), *Model Tax Convention on Income and on Capital 2014 (Full Version)*, OECD Publishing, Paris, http://dx.doi.org/10.1787/9789264239081-en.

OECD (2015b), *Making Dispute Resolution Mechanisms More Effective, Action 14 - 2015 Final Report*, OECD Publishing, Paris, http://dx.doi.org/10.1787/9789264241633-en.

Part D

Implementation of MAP Agreements

[D.1] Implement all MAP agreements

> Jurisdictions should implement any agreement reached in MAP discussions, including by making appropriate adjustments to the tax assessed in transfer pricing cases.

149. In order to provide full certainty to taxpayers and the jurisdictions, it is essential that all MAP agreements are implemented by the competent authorities concerned.

Legal framework to implement MAP agreements

150. If the United States' competent authority enters into a MAP agreement with the other competent authority concerned, the tentative agreement reached is communicated to the taxpayer for consideration along with any explanation of all steps taxpayers may need to take to have the agreement implemented. In section 9.02 of the United States' MAP guidance it is stipulated that taxpayers have the opportunity to either accept or reject the agreement reached.[1] This both applies to agreements reached through MAP or following the application of an arbitration procedure under the relevant tax treaty as a final stage to the MAP. In case taxpayers accept the MAP agreement, the United States' competent authority subsequently will, as detailed in section 9.04 of its MAP guidance, instruct the IRS to implement such agreement by means of a letter and a disposition memorandum to the appropriate IRS office or service centre. This letter explains the details of the agreement reached and instructs the recipient to implement the MAP agreement as described in the disposition memorandum. That office or service centre is subsequently required to implement the MAP agreement. If taxpayers reject the MAP agreement, the United States' competent authority will close the case. Taxpayers may then pursue domestic remedies, if still available. Section 9.02 of the MAP guidance allows the United States' competent authority to deem that a taxpayer did not accept a MAP agreement if they do not timely give their consent. It, however, is not specified within what timeframe such consent should be given.

151. The United States implements all MAP agreements reached, provided that taxpayer accepted the agreement. MAP agreements are thereby implemented notwithstanding domestic time limits, unless such time limits are not waived under the applicable tax treaty. In such situation, implementation of a MAP agreement is subject to statute of limitations under domestic law, which may prevent the IRS from implementing a MAP agreement that requires an upward adjustment to the tax liability in the United States. To avoid that MAP agreements cannot be implemented due to domestic statute of limitations and to protect taxpayers' rights on a refund of taxes or on a potential credit, the United States allows taxpayers to file protective MAP claims. Section 11 of its MAP guidance details the rules and requirements for the filing of such protective claims.

Practical application

152. The United States reported that all MAP agreements, once accepted by taxpayers, have been implemented and that it is not aware of any MAP agreements that were not implemented since 1 January 2014. It, however, has not implemented a mechanism to keep track on whether all MAP agreements reached are actually implemented.

153. In general peers indicated not being aware of MAP agreements that were not implemented by the United States. Two peers specifically mentioned that the United States' competent authority is very efficient in implementing MAP agreements. One peer, however, noted that at the time of its input two MAP agreements reached in July 2016 had not been implemented due to the tentative status of the agreement in the United States. For one case, closing procedures have since been initiated. For the second case the United States responded that, due to highly unusual circumstances that arose after negotiations but before exchanging letters of agreement, the United States re-evaluated the case. The United States will provide a formal written explanation to the peer stating its reasons to enter into further negotiations after a tentative agreement already had been reached.

Anticipated modifications

154. The United States did not indicate that it anticipates any modifications in relation to element D.1.

Conclusion

	Areas for Improvement	Recommendations
D.1	-	As the United States has implemented all MAP agreements thus far, it should continue to implement all future agreements if the conditions for such implementation are fulfilled. In addition, to ensure that all MAP agreements continue to be implemented if the conditions for such implementation are fulfilled, the United States could introduce a tracking system.

[D.2] Implement all MAP agreements on a timely basis

> Agreements reached by competent authorities through the MAP process should be implemented on a timely basis.

155. Delay of implementation of MAP agreements may lead to adverse financial consequences for both taxpayers and competent authorities. To avoid this and to increase certainty for all parties involved, it is important that the implementation of any MAP agreement is not obstructed by procedural and/or statutory delays in the jurisdictions concerned.

Theoretical timeframe for implementing mutual agreements

156. In its domestic legislation and/or administrative framework, the United States does not have in place a timeframe for implementation of mutual agreements reached. This regards both the situation in which the MAP agreement leads to additional tax to be paid or to a refund of tax in the United States. Furthermore, the United States' MAP guidance does not include information in relation hereto.

Practical application

157. The United States reported that all MAP agreements, once accepted by taxpayers, have been implemented and that it is not aware of any MAP agreements that were not implemented on a timely basis since 1 January 2014. As discussed under element D.1, the United States has not implemented a mechanism to keep track on whether all MAP agreements reached are actually implemented, and whether in a timely basis.

158. Peers did in general not indicate experiencing any problems with the United States regarding the implementation of MAP agreements on a timely basis. Two peers specifically mentioned that the United States' competent authority is very efficient in implementing MAP agreements. However, three peers raised particular issues regarding the timely implementation of MAP agreements. One peer noted that implementation of MAP agreements may take substantial time in the United States due to formal administrative and policy regulations. Another peer noted that implementation of MAP agreements by the TAIT team can be delayed due to the fact that implementation is dependent on the – time-consuming and complicated– procedure for non-residents to obtain a Tax Identification Number. The third peer reported that in its view the internal processes in the United States for management oversight/sign-offs of competent authority decisions seem to be unduly extensive, which can delay timely implementation of MAP agreements. Furthermore, one taxpayer provided input and mentioned that implementation of MAP agreements appear to be long.

Anticipated modifications

159. The United States did not indicate that it anticipates any modifications in relation to element D.2.

Conclusion

	Areas for Improvement	Recommendations
[D.2]	-	As it has done thus far, the United States should continue to implement all MAP agreements on a timely basis if the conditions for such implementation are fulfilled.

[D.3] Include Article 25(2), second sentence, of the *OECD Model Tax Convention* in tax treaties or alternative provisions in Article 9(1) and Article 7(2)

> Jurisdictions should either (i) provide in their tax treaties that any mutual agreement reached through MAP shall be implemented notwithstanding any time limits in their domestic law, or (ii) be willing to accept alternative treaty provisions that limit the time during which a Contracting Party may make an adjustment pursuant to Article 9(1) or Article 7(2), in order to avoid late adjustments with respect to which MAP relief will not be available.

160. In order to provide full certainty to taxpayers it is essential that the implementation of MAP agreements is not obstructed by any time limits in the domestic law of the jurisdictions concerned. Such certainty can be provided by either including the equivalent of Article 25(2), second sentence, of the *OECD Model Tax Convention* (OECD, 2015) in tax treaties, or alternatively, setting a time limit in Article 9(1) and Article 7(2) for making adjustments to avoid that late adjustments obstruct granting of MAP relief.

Legal framework and current situation of the United States' tax treaties

161. As discussed under element D.1, the United States has under its domestic legislation a statute of limitation for claiming of refunds. This statute of limitation, however, is overruled if a tax treaty includes a provision equivalent to Article 25(2), second sentence, of the *OECD Model Tax Convention* (OECD, 2015), stipulating that MAP agreements are implemented notwithstanding any time limits in the jurisdiction's domestic legislation. Furthermore, the United States did not reserve in the Commentary to Article 25 of the OECD Model Convention (OECD, 2015) the right not to incorporate the second sentence of Article 25(2) in its tax treaties. In fact, the U.S. Model Tax Convention, which is the baseline text used by the U.S. Treasury Department when it negotiations income tax treaties includes a provision equivalent to Article 25(2), second sentence, of the *OECD Model Tax Convention* (OECD, 2015).

162. Out of the United States' 60 tax treaties, 41 contain a provision equivalent to Article 25(2), second sentence, of the *OECD Model Tax Convention* (OECD, 2015) that any mutual agreement reached through MAP shall be implemented notwithstanding any time limits in their domestic law. For the remaining 19 treaties, the following analysis is made:

- Three treaties do not contain a provision concerning the implementation of MAP agreements, which are considered not having the equivalent of Article 25(2), second sentence, of the *OECD Model Tax Convention* (OECD, 2015). One of these treaties concerns the treaty with the former USSR;

- Five treaties contain a provision on the implementation of MAP agreements, but these treaties do not include wording on the implementation of MAP agreements notwithstanding any time limits in the domestic law of the contracting states.[2] These five treaties therefore are considered not having the equivalent of Article 25(2), second sentence, of the *OECD Model Tax Convention* (OECD, 2015);

- Seven treaties include a variation to the provision of Article 25(2), second sentence, of the *OECD Model Tax Convention* (OECD, 2015) whereby the actual implementation of a MAP agreement is dependent on the notification of a MAP request to the other competent authority involved within a certain term. These seven treaties therefore are considered not to be a full equivalent of Article 25(2), second sentence, of the *OECD Model Tax Convention* (OECD, 2015);

- One treaty includes a variation to the provision of Article 25(2), second sentence, of the *OECD Model Tax Convention* (OECD, 2015) where the actual implementation of a MAP agreement is dependent on the notification of a MAP request to the other competent authority involved within a certain term. This treaty therefore is considered not having the full equivalent of Article 25(2), second sentence, of the *OECD Model Tax Convention* (OECD, 2015); and

- Three treaties include the equivalent provision to Article 25(2), second sentence, of the *OECD Model Tax Convention* (OECD, 2015), but also requires that domestic statute of limitations are interrupted or are supplemented with the wording: *except such limitations as apply for the purposes of giving effect to such agreement*. Although the United States uses no statute of limitations for implementing MAP agreements and interprets this provision as not limiting the implementation of MAP agreements, such statute of limitation may be in existence in the domestic legislation of the treaty partner. These three treaties therefore are considered not having the full equivalent of Article 25(2), second sentence, of the *OECD Model Tax Convention* (OECD, 2015).

163. Further to the above, the treaty with Switzerland is one of the three treaties that does not include the equivalent of Article 25(2), second sentence, of the *OECD Model Tax Convention* (OECD, 2015). It also has no timeframe for submission of MAP requests. The United States' unilateral technical explanation to that treaty addresses that Switzerland will apply a 10-year notification period under the treaty for Swiss federal and cantonal taxes. In other words, Switzerland only provides for relief of double taxation following a MAP agreement, where the relevant MAP request was submitted within this 10-year period. For that reason the United States also uses a 10-year notification period for submissions of MAP requests. In principle, using such notification period may lead to a situation in which access to MAP is denied. Furthermore, even if in such situation there may be access to the MAP, there is a risk that MAP agreements are under that treaty not implemented notwithstanding the domestic statute of limitations.

Anticipated modifications

164. For those treaties that do not contain a provision equivalent to Article 25(2), first sentence, of the *OECD Model Tax Convention*, the United States indicated that it intends to implement element D.3 for all its existing tax treaties. As 1 of the 19 treaties regards the treaty with the former USSR, this treaty can in any case not be modified so as to be compliant with element D.3. For the other treaties the United States indicated that it would conduct any ongoing negotiations or enter into future negotiations with a current or prospective treaty partner with a view to be compliant with element D.3.

165. Some peers noted that they are either conducting negotiations with the United States or envisaging such negotiations with a view to be compliant with the relevant elements of the Action 14 Minimum Standard.

Conclusion

	Areas for Improvement	Recommendations
[D.3]	19 out of 60 tax treaties contain neither a provision that is equivalent to Article 25(2), second sentence of the *OECD Model Tax Convention* (OECD, 2015) nor the alternative provisions in both Article 9(1) and Article 7(2).	Where treaties do not include the equivalent of Article 25(2), second sentence, of the *OECD Model Tax Convention* (OECD, 2015), or the alternatives provided in Article 9(1) and Article 7(2), the United States should request the inclusion of the required provision or be willing to accept the inclusion of both alternative provisions. Specifically with respect to the treaty with the former USSR, the United States should, once it enters into negotiations with the jurisdictions for which it applies the treaty, request the inclusion of the required provision or its alternatives. In addition, the United States should maintain its stated intention to include the required provision, or be willing to accept the inclusion of both alternative provisions, in all future treaties.

Notes

1. In section 9.03 of the MAP guidance it is further clarified that if a MAP agreement concerns multiple issues, taxpayers have the possibility not to accept all issues agreed on.

2. It is noted that for these some of these treaties, the unilateral technical explanation by the United States mentions that a refund of taxes or a tax credit following a MAP agreement shall be granted notwithstanding procedural barriers otherwise existing in the laws of the contracting states. As this, however, is not included in the treaty and the technical explanation is not binding on both contracting states, there is no general obligation for both competent authorities to implement MAP agreements notwithstanding domestic time limits.

Bibliography

OECD (2015), *Model Tax Convention on Income and on Capital 2014 (Full Version)*, OECD Publishing, Paris, http://dx.doi.org/10.1787/9789264239081-en.

Summary

	Areas for Improvement	Recommendations
Part A: Preventing disputes		
[A.1]	Two out of 60 tax treaties do not contain a provision that is equivalent to Article 25(3), first sentence, of the *OECD Model Tax Convention* (OECD, 2015)	Where treaties do not include the equivalent of Article 25(3), first sentence, of the *OECD Model Tax Convention* (OECD, 2015), the United States should request the inclusion of the required provision via bilateral negotiations. Specifically with respect to the treaty with the former USSR, the United States should, once it enters into negotiations with the jurisdictions for which it applies the treaty, request the inclusion of the required provision. In addition, the United States should maintain its stated intention to include the required provision in all future treaties.
[A.2]	-	The United States should continue to provide for roll-back of bilateral APAs in appropriate cases as it has done thus far.
Part B: Availability and access to MAP		
[B.1]	Three out of 60 tax treaties do not contain a provision that is the equivalent of Article 25(1), first sentence of the *OECD Model Tax Convention* (OECD, 2015), either as it read prior to the adoption of the Action 14 final report (OECD, 2015b) or as amended by that final report.	Where treaties do not include the equivalent of Article 25(1) of the *OECD Model Tax Convention* (OECD, 2015), the United States should request the inclusion of the required provision via bilateral negotiations. This concerns a provision that is equivalent to Article 25(1), first sentence of the *OECD Model Tax Convention* either: a) As amended in the Action 14 final report (OECD, 2015); or b) As it read prior to the adoption of the Action 14 final report (OECD, 2015). In addition, the United States should maintain its stated intention to include the required provision in all future treaties.
[B.2]	The United States has in place a process to notify and consult the other competent authority in cases its competent authority considered the objection raised in a MAP request as not justified. However, because for the period under review no such cases have occurred during the Review Period, it was not possible to assess whether the notification and consultation process is applied in practice.	
[B.3]	-	As the United States has thus far granted access to the MAP in eligible transfer pricing cases, it should continue granting access for these cases.
[B.4]	-	As the United States thus far has granted access to the MAP in eligible cases concerning whether the conditions for the application of a treaty anti-abuse provision have been met or whether the application of a domestic law anti-abuse provision is in conflict with the provisions of a treaty, it should continue granting access for these cases.

	Areas for Improvement	Recommendations
[B.5]	-	As the United States has thus far granted access to the MAP in eligible cases, even if there was an audit settlement between the IRS and the taxpayer, it should continue granting access for these cases.
[B.6]	-	As the United States has thus far not limited access to the MAP in eligible cases when taxpayers have complied with the United States' information and documentation requirements for MAP requests, it should continue this practice.
[B.7]	14 out of 60 tax treaties do not contain a provision that is equivalent to Article 25(3), second sentence, of the *OECD Model Tax Convention* (OECD, 2015).	Where treaties do not include the equivalent of Article 25(3), second sentence, of the *OECD Model Tax Convention* (OECD, 2015), the United States should request the inclusion of the required provision via bilateral negotiations. Specifically with respect to the treaty with the former USSR, the United States should, once it enters into negotiations with the jurisdictions for which it applies those treaties, request the inclusion of the required provision. In addition, the United States should maintain its stated intention to include the required provision in all future treaties.
[B.8]	MAP guidance is comprehensive and available, but some further clarity could still be provided.	Although not required by the Action 14 Minimum Standard, in order to further improve the level of clarity of its MAP guidance, the United States could consider including information on: o Whether MAP is available in cases of multilateral disputes; and o The process how MAP agreements are implemented in terms of steps to be taken and timing of these steps, including actions to be taken by taxpayers and the timeframe for giving consent to the MAP agreement reached.
[B.9]	-	The United States should ensure that future updates of its MAP guidance are made publically available and easily accessible and that its MAP profile, published on the shared public platform, is updated if needed.
[B.10]	-	-
Part C: Resolution of MAP cases		
[C.1]	14 out of 60 tax treaties do not contain a provision that is equivalent to Article 25(2), first sentence, of the *OECD Model Tax Convention*.	Where treaties do not include the equivalent of Article 25(2), first sentence, of the *OECD Model Tax Convention* (OECD, 2015), the United States should request the inclusion of the required provision via bilateral negotiations. In addition, the United States should maintain its stated intention to include the required provision in all future treaties.
[C.2]	The United States submitted timely comprehensive MAP statistics and indicated they have been matched with its MAP partners. The year 2016 was the first year for which MAP statistics were reported under the new MAP Statistics Reporting Framework. These statistics were only recently submitted by most jurisdictions that committed themselves to the implementation of the Action 14 Minimum Standard and some still need to be submitted or confirmed. Given this state of play, it was not yet possible to assess whether the United States' MAP statistics match those of its treaty partners as reported by the latter. Within the context of the state of play outlined above and in relation to the MAP statistics provided by the United States, it resolved during the Reporting Period 4.54% (eight out of 176 cases) of its post-2015 cases in 4.44 months on average. In that regard, the United States is recommended to seek to resolve the remaining 95.36% of the post-	

	Areas for Improvement	Recommendations
	2015 cases pending on 31 December 2016 (168 cases) within a timeframe that results in an average timeframe of 24 months for all post-2015 cases.	
[C.3]	As the United States resolved MAP cases in 30.87 months on average, there may be a risk that post-2015 cases are not resolved within the average of 24 months, which is the pursued average for resolving MAP cases received on or after 1 January 2016 and which might indicate that the available resources in the United States' competent authority are not adequately used.	The United States should ensure that the resources available for the competent authority function are adequately used in order to resolve MAP cases in a timely, efficient and effective manner.
[C.4]	-	As it has done thus far, the United States should continue to ensure that its competent authority has the authority, and uses that authority in practice, to resolve MAP cases without being dependent on approval or direction from the tax administration personnel directly involved in the adjustments at issue.-
[C.5]	-	As it has done thus far, the United States should continue to use appropriate performance indicators.
[C.6]	-	-
Part D: Implementation of MAP agreements		
[D.1]	-	As the United States has implemented all MAP agreements thus far, it should continue to implement all future agreements if the conditions for such implementation are fulfilled. In addition, to ensure that all MAP agreements continue to be implemented if the conditions for such implementation are fulfilled, the United States could introduce a tracking system.
[D.2]	-	As it has done thus far, the United States should continue to implement all MAP agreements on a timely basis if the conditions for such implementation are fulfilled.
[D.3]	19 out of 60 tax treaties contain neither a provision that is equivalent to Article 25(2), second sentence of the *OECD Model Tax Convention* (OECD, 2015), nor the alternative provisions in both Article 9(1) and Article 7(2).	Where treaties do not include the equivalent of Article 25(2), second sentence, of the *OECD Model Tax Convention* (OECD, 2015), or include the alternatives provided in Article 9(1) and Article 7(2), the United States should request the inclusion of the required provision or be willing to accept the inclusion of both alternative provisions. Specifically with respect to the treaty with the former USSR, the United States should, once it enters into negotiations with the jurisdictions for which it applies the treaty, request the inclusion of the required provision. In addition, the United States should maintain its stated intention to include the required provision, or be willing to accept the inclusion of both alternative provisions, in all future treaties.

Annex A
Tax treaty network of United States

Column 1	Column 2	Action 25(1) of the OECD Model Tax Convention ("MTC")			Article 9(2) of the OECD MTC	Anti-abuse	Article 25(2) of the OECD MTC		Article 25(3) of the OECD MTC		Arbitration
		B.1			B.3	B.4	C.1	D.3	A.1	B.7	C.6
		Column 3	Column 4		Column 5	Column 6	Column 7	Column 8	Column 9	Column 10	Column 11
Treaty partner	DTC in force?	Is Art. 25(1), first sentence included?	Is Art. 25(1), second sentence included?		Is Art. 9(2) included?	Inclusion provision that MAP Article will not be available in cases where your jurisdiction is of the assessment that there is an abuse of the DTC or of the domestic tax law?	Is Art. 25(2) first sentence included?	Is Art. 25(2) second sentence included?	Is Art. 25(3) first sentence included?	Is Art. 25(3) second sentence included?	Inclusion arbitration provision?
		If yes, submission to either competent authority (new Art. 25(1), first sentence)	If no, please state reasons			If no, will your CA accept a taxpayer's request for MAP in relation to such cases?		If no, alternative provision in Art. 7 & 9 OECD MTC?			
	Y = yes	E = yes, either CAs	Y = yes		Y = yes	Y = yes	Y = yes	Y = yes	Y = yes	Y = yes	Y = yes if yes:
	N = signed pending ratification	O = yes, only one CA	i = no, no such provision		i = no, but access will be given to TP cases	i = no and such cases will be accepted for MAP	N = no	i = no, but have Art 7 equivalent	N = no	N = no	N = no
		N = No	ii = no, different period		ii = no and access will not be given to TP cases	ii = no but such cases will not be accepted for MAP		ii = no, but have Art 9 equivalent			i-Art. 25(5)
			iii = no, starting point for computing the 3 year period is different					iii = no, but have both Art 7 & 9 equivalent			
			iv = no, others reasons					N = no and no equivalent of Art 7 and 9			
Armenia	Y	O	i		i	i	N	N	N	N	N
Australia	Y	O	Y		Y	i	N	Y	Y	N	N
Austria	Y	O	i		Y	i	Y	Y	Y	Y	N

Annex A - Tax Treaty Network of United States

		Action 25(1) of the OECD Model Tax Convention ("MTC")		Article 9(2) of the OECD MTC	Anti-abuse	Article 25(2) of the OECD MTC		Article 25(3) of the OECD MTC		Arbitration
		B.1		B.3	B.4	C.1	D.3	A.1	B.7	C.6
Column 1	Column 2	Column 3	Column 4	Column 5	Column 6	Column 7	Column 8	Column 9	Column 10	Column 11
Treaty partner	DTC in force?	Is Art. 25(1), first sentence included? / If yes, submission to either competent authority (new Art. 25(1), first sentence)	Is Art. 25(1), second sentence included? / If no, please state reasons	Is Art. 9(2) included?	Inclusion provision that MAP Article will not be available in cases where your jurisdiction is of the assessment that there is an abuse of the DTC or of the domestic tax law? / If no, will your CA accept a taxpayer's request for MAP in relation to such cases?	Is Art. 25(2) first sentence included?	Is Art. 25(2) second sentence included? / If no, alternative provision in Art. 7 & 9 OECD MTC?	Is Art. 25(3) first sentence included?	Is Art. 25(3) second sentence included?	Inclusion arbitration provision?
Azerbaijan	Y	O	--	--	--	N	N	N	N	N
Bangladesh	Y	E	--	Y	--	Y	Y	Y	Y	N
Barbados	Y	O	--	Y	--	Y	Y	Y	Y	N
Belarus	Y	O	--	--	--	N	N	N	N	N
Belgium	Y	E	Y	Y	--	Y	Y	Y	N	Y (ii)
Bulgaria	Y	E	--	Y	--	Y	Y	Y	Y	N
Canada	Y	O	--	--	--	Y	N	Y	Y	Y (ii)
Chile	N	O	Y	Y	--	Y	Y	Y	N	N
China	Y	O	Y	Y	--	Y	Y	Y	Y	N
Cyprus*	Y	O	--	--	--	N	Y	Y	Y	N
Czech Republic	Y	O	Y	Y	--	Y	Y	Y	Y	N
Denmark	Y	O	--	Y	--	Y	Y	Y	Y	N
Egypt	Y	O	--	--	--	N	Y	Y	N	N
Estonia	Y	E	Y	Y	--	Y	Y	Y	Y	N
Finland	Y	O	--	Y	--	Y	N	Y	Y	N

ANNEX A - TAX TREATY NETWORK OF UNITED STATES

Column 1	Column 2	Action 25(1) of the OECD Model Tax Convention ("MTC")		Article 9(2) of the OECD MTC	Anti-abuse	Article 25(2) of the OECD MTC		Article 25(3) of the OECD MTC		Arbitration
		B.1		B.3	B.4	C.1	D.3	A.1	B.7	C.6
Treaty partner	Column 2	Column 3	Column 4	Column 5	Column 6	Column 7	Column 8	Column 9	Column 10	Column 11
	DTC in force?	Is Art. 25(1), first sentence included? / If yes, submission to either competent authority (new Art. 25(1), first sentence)	Is Art. 25(1), second sentence included? / If no, please state reasons	Is Art. 9(2) included?	Inclusion provision that MAP Article will not be available in cases where your jurisdiction is of the assessment that there is an abuse of the DTC or of the domestic tax law? / If no, will your CA accept a taxpayer's request for MAP in relation to such cases?	Is Art. 25(2) first sentence included?	Is Art. 25(2) second sentence included? / If no, alternative provision in Art. 7 & 9 OECD MTC?	Is Art. 25(3) first sentence included?	Is Art. 25(3) second sentence included?	Inclusion arbitration provision?
France	Y	O	Y	--	--	Y	Y	Y	Y	Y / ii
Georgia	Y	O	--	--	--	N	N	N	N	N
Germany	Y	O	ii (4 years)	Y	--	Y	Y	Y	Y	Y / ii
Greece	Y	N	--	--	--	N	N	Y	N	N
Hungary	N	O	i (6 years)	Y	--	Y	N	Y	Y	N
Iceland	Y	E	--	Y	--	Y	Y	Y	Y	N
India	Y	O	Y	Y	--	Y	Y	Y	Y	N
Indonesia	Y	O	Y	Y	--	Y	Y	Y	Y	N
Ireland	Y	E	--	Y	--	Y	Y	Y	Y	Y / iii
Israel	Y	O	--	--	--	N	Y	Y	N	N
Italy	Y	O	Y	--	--	Y	Y	Y	Y	Y / iii
Jamaica	Y	O/E	--	--	--	Y	N	Y	Y	N
Japan	Y	O	Y	--	--	Y	N	Y	Y	Y / ii
Kazakhstan	Y	O	--	Y	--	Y	Y	Y	Y	Y / iii
Korea	Y	O	--	--	--	N	N	Y	N	N

ANNEX A - TAX TREATY NETWORK OF UNITED STATES

| Column 1 | Column 2 | Action 25(1) of the OECD Model Tax Convention ("MTC") | | Article 9(2) of the OECD MTC | Anti-abuse | Article 25(2) of the OECD MTC | | Article 25(3) of the OECD MTC | | Arbitration |
| | | B.1 / Column 3 | Column 4 | B.3 / Column 5 | B.4 / Column 6 | C.1 / Column 7 | D.3 / Column 8 | A.1 / Column 9 | B.7 / Column 10 | C.6 / Column 11 |
Treaty partner	DTC in force?	Is Art. 25(1), first sentence included? If yes, submission to either competent authority (new Art. 25(1), first sentence)	Is Art. 25(1), second sentence included? If no, please state reasons	Is Art. 9(2) included?	Inclusion provision that MAP Article will not be available in cases where your jurisdiction is of the assessment that there is an abuse of the DTC or of the domestic tax law? If no, will your CA accept a taxpayer's request for MAP in relation to such cases?	Is Art. 25(2) first sentence included?	Is Art. 25(2) second sentence included? If no, alternative provision in Art. 7 & 9 OECD MTC?	Is Art. 25(3) first sentence included?	Is Art. 25(3) second sentence included?	Inclusion arbitration provision?
Kyrgyzstan	Y	O	i	i	i	N	N	N	N	N
Latvia	Y	E	Y	Y	i	Y	Y	Y	Y	N
Lithuania	Y	E	Y	Y	i	Y	Y	Y	Y	N
Luxembourg	Y	O	i	Y	i	Y	Y	Y	Y	N
Malta	Y	E	i	Y	i	Y	Y	Y	Y	N
Mexico	Y	O	i	i	i	N	N	Y	Y	N
Moldova	Y	O	i	i	i	N	N	N	N	N
Morocco	Y	O	i	i	i	N	Y	Y	N	N
Netherlands	Y	O	i	Y	i	Y	N	Y	N	Y
New Zealand	Y	O	Y	Y	i	Y	Y	Y	Y	N
Norway	Y	O	i	i	i	N	Y	Y	N	N
Pakistan	Y	N	i	i	i	N	N	N	N	N
Philippines	Y	O	i	i	i	N	N	Y	N	N
Poland	N	O	Y	Y	i	Y	Y	Y	Y	N

ANNEX A - TAX TREATY NETWORK OF UNITED STATES

		Action 25(1) of the OECD Model Tax Convention ("MTC")		Article 9(2) of the OECD MTC	Anti-abuse	Article 25(2) of the OECD MTC		Article 25(3) of the OECD MTC		Arbitration
		B.1		B.3	B.4	C.1	D.3	A.1	B.7	C.6
Column 1	Column 2	Column 3	Column 4	Column 5	Column 6	Column 7	Column 8	Column 9	Column 10	Column 11
Treaty partner	DTC in force?	Is Art. 25(1), first sentence included? / If yes, submission to either competent authority (new Art. 25(1), first sentence)	Is Art. 25(1), second sentence included? / If no, please state reasons	Is Art. 9(2) included?	Inclusion provision that MAP Article will not be available in cases where your jurisdiction is of the assessment that there is an abuse of the DTC or of the domestic tax law? / If no, will your CA accept a taxpayer's request for MAP in relation to such cases?	Is Art. 25(2) first sentence included?	Is Art. 25(2) second sentence included? / If no, alternative provision in Art. 7 & 9 OECD MTC?	Is Art. 25(3) first sentence included?	Is Art. 25(3) second sentence included?	Inclusion arbitration provision?
Portugal	Y	O	ii (5 years)	Y	i	Y	Y	Y	Y	N
Romania	Y	O	i	i	i	N	N	Y	N	N
Russia	Y	O	i	i	i	Y	Y	Y	Y	N
Slovak Republic	Y	O	Y	Y	i	Y	Y	Y	Y	N
Slovenia	Y	O	ii (5 years)	Y	i	Y	Y	Y	Y	N
South Africa	Y	E	Y	Y	i	Y	Y	Y	Y	N
Spain	Y	O	ii (5 years)	Y	i	Y	Y	Y	Y	Y
Sri Lanka	Y	O	i	Y	i	Y	Y	Y	Y	N
Sweden	Y	O	i	Y	i	Y	Y	Y	Y	N
Switzerland	Y	O	i	i	i	Y	N	Y	Y	Y
Tajikistan	Y	O	i	i	i	N	N	N	N	N
Thailand	Y	O	Y	Y	i	Y	N	Y	Y	N
Trinidad and Tobago	Y	N	i	i	i	N	N	Y	N	N

ANNEX A - TAX TREATY NETWORK OF UNITED STATES

Column 1	Column 2	Action 25(1) of the OECD Model Tax Convention ("MTC")		Article 9(2) of the OECD MTC	Anti-abuse	Article 25(2) of the OECD MTC		Article 25(3) of the OECD MTC		Arbitration
		B.1		B.3	B.4	C.1	D.3	A.1	B.7	C.6
		Column 3	Column 4	Column 5	Column 6	Column 7	Column 8	Column 9	Column 10	Column 11
Treaty partner	DTC in force?	Is Art. 25(1), first sentence included? If yes, submission to either competent authority (new Art. 25(1), first sentence)	Is Art. 25(1), second sentence included? If no, please state reasons	Is Art. 9(2) included?	Inclusion provision that MAP Article will not be available in cases where your jurisdiction is of the assessment that there is an abuse of the DTC or of the domestic tax law? If no, will your CA accept a taxpayer's request for MAP in relation to such cases?	Is Art. 25(2) first sentence included?	Is Art. 25(2) second sentence included? If no, alternative provision in Art. 7 & 9 OECD MTC?	Is Art. 25(3) first sentence included?	Is Art. 25(3) second sentence included?	Inclusion arbitration provision?
Tunisia	Y	O	i	Y	i	Y	Y	Y	Y	N
Turkey	Y	O	i	Y	i	Y	N	Y	Y	N
Turkmenistan	Y	O	i	i	i	N	N	N	N	N
Ukraine	Y	O	i	Y	i	Y	Y	Y	Y	N
United Kingdom	Y	O	Y	Y	i	Y	N	Y	Y	N
Uzbekistan	Y	O	i	i	i	N	N	N	N	N
Venezuela	Y	E	i	Y	i	Y	N	Y	Y	N
Viet-Nam	N	O	Y	Y	i	Y	Y	Y	Y	N

Annex B
MAP Statistics pre-2016 cases

Category of cases	No. Of pre-2016 cases in MAP inventory on 1 January 2016	Number of pre-2016 cases closed during the reporting period by outcome:										No. Of pre-2016 cases remaining in on MAP inventory on 31 December 2016	Average time taken (in months) for closing pre-2016 cases during the reporting period
		Denied MAP access	Objection is not justified	Withdrawn by taxpayer	Unilateral relief granted	Resolved via domestic remedy	Agreement fully eliminating double taxation / fully resolving taxation not in accordance with tax treaty	Agreement partially eliminating double taxation / partially resolving taxation not in accordance with tax treaty	Agreement that there is no taxation not in accordance with tax treaty	No agreement including agreement to disagree	Any other outcome		
Column 1	Column 2	Column 3	Column 4	Column 5	Column 6	Column 7	Column 8	Column 9	Column 10	Column 11	Column 12	Column 13	Column 14
Attribution/ Allocation	716	0	0	6	20	0	100	5	0	0	11	574	32.20
Others	256	0	1	3	7	5	17	0	0	0	2	221	31.53
Total	972	0	1	9	27	5	117	5	0	0	13	795	32.07

Notes:
Number of pre-2016 cases in MAP inventory on 1 January 2016 exceeds the amount of ending inventory reported in 2015 due to addition of cases that were received by the U.S. competent authority on or after 1 January 2016 but were received by the applicable treaty partner before 1 January 2016.

Annex C
MAP Statistics post-2015 cases

Treaty partner	No. Of post-2015 cases in MAP inventory on 1 January 2016	No. Of post-2015 cases started during the reporting period	Number of post-2015 cases closed during the reporting period by outcome:										No. Of post-2015 cases remaining in MAP inventory on 31 December 2016	Average time taken (in months) for closing post-2015 cases during the reporting period
			Denied MAP access	Objection is not justified	Withdrawn by taxpayer	Unilateral relief granted	Resolved via domestic remedy	Agreement fully eliminating double taxation eliminated / fully resolving taxation not in accordance with tax treaty	Agreement partially eliminating double taxation / partially resolving taxation not in accordance with tax treaty	Agreement that there is no taxation not in accordance with tax treaty	No agreement including agreement to disagree	Any other outcome		
Column 1	Column 2	Column 3	Column 4	Column 5	Column 6	Column 7	Column 8	Column 9	Column 10	Column 11	Column 12	Column 13	Column 14	Column 14
Attribution/ Allocation	0	128	0	0	1	0	0	2	0	0	0	0	125	3.8
Others	0	48	0	2	2	0	0	1	0	0	0	0	43	4.82
Total	0	176	0	2	3	0	0	3	0	0	0	0	168	4.44

Notes

We were unable to confirm post-2015 cases started during the reporting period with two jurisdictions included in Treaty Partners (de minimis rule applies) due to lack of contact with the relevant jurisdiction.

Glossary

Action 14 Minimum Standard	The minimum standard as agreed upon in the final report on Action 14: Making Dispute Resolution Mechanisms More Effective
APA guidance	Rev. Proc. 2015-41
LOB Article	Limitations on benefits article
Look-back period	Period starting from 1 January 2014 for which the United States wished to provide information and requested peer input
MAP guidance	Rev. Proc. 2015-40
MAP Statistics Reporting Framework	Rules for reporting of MAP statistics as agreed by the FTA MAP Forum
OECD Model Tax Convention	*OECD Model Tax Convention* on Income and on Capital as it read on 15 July 2014
Pre-2016 cases	MAP cases in a competent authority's inventory that are pending resolution on 31 December 2015
Post-2015 cases	MAP cases that are received by a competent authority from the taxpayer on or after 1 January 2016
Reporting period	Period for reporting MAP statistics that started on 1 January 2016 and that ended on 31 December 2016
Terms of Reference	Terms of reference to monitor and review the implementing of the BEPS Action 14 Minimum Standard to make dispute resolution mechanisms more effective
U.S. Model Tax Convention	United States Model Income Tax Convention as it read on 17 February 2016

ORGANISATION FOR ECONOMIC CO-OPERATION AND DEVELOPMENT

The OECD is a unique forum where governments work together to address the economic, social and environmental challenges of globalisation. The OECD is also at the forefront of efforts to understand and to help governments respond to new developments and concerns, such as corporate governance, the information economy and the challenges of an ageing population. The Organisation provides a setting where governments can compare policy experiences, seek answers to common problems, identify good practice and work to co-ordinate domestic and international policies.

The OECD member countries are: Australia, Austria, Belgium, Canada, Chile, the Czech Republic, Denmark, Estonia, Finland, France, Germany, Greece, Hungary, Iceland, Ireland, Israel, Italy, Japan, Korea, Latvia, Luxembourg, Mexico, the Netherlands, New Zealand, Norway, Poland, Portugal, the Slovak Republic, Slovenia, Spain, Sweden, Switzerland, Turkey, the United Kingdom and the United States. The European Union takes part in the work of the OECD.

OECD Publishing disseminates widely the results of the Organisation's statistics gathering and research on economic, social and environmental issues, as well as the conventions, guidelines and standards agreed by its members.

www.ingramcontent.com/pod-product-compliance
Lightning Source LLC
Chambersburg PA
CBHW082358220526
45470CB00008B/2782

OECD/G20 Base Erosion and Profit Shifting Project

Making Dispute Resolution More Effective – MAP Peer Review Report, United States (Stage 1)

INCLUSIVE FRAMEWORK ON BEPS: ACTION 14

Addressing base erosion and profit shifting is a key priority of governments around the globe. In 2013, OECD and G20 countries, working together on an equal footing, adopted a 15-point Action Plan to address BEPS. Beyond securing revenues by realigning taxation with economic activities and value creation, the OECD/G20 BEPS Project aims to create a single set of consensus-based international tax rules to address BEPS, and hence to protect tax bases while offering increased certainty and predictability to taxpayers. In 2015, the OECD and G20 established an Inclusive Framework on BEPS to allow interested countries and jurisdictions to work with OECD and G20 members to develop standards on BEPS related issues and reviewing and monitoring the implementation of the whole BEPS Package.

Under Action 14, countries have committed to implement a minimum standard to strengthen the effectiveness and efficiency of the mutual agreement procedure (MAP). The MAP is included in Article 25 of the OECD Model Tax Convention and commits countries to endeavour to resolve disputes related to the interpretation and application of tax treaties. The Action 14 Minimum Standard has been translated into specific terms of reference and a methodology for the peer review and monitoring process. The minimum standard is complemented by a set of best practices.

The peer review process is conducted in two stages. Stage 1 assesses countries against the terms of reference of the minimum standard according to an agreed schedule of review. Stage 2 focuses on monitoring the follow-up of any recommendations resulting from jurisdictions' stage 1 peer review report. This report reflects the outcome of the stage 1 peer review of the implementation of the Action 14 Minimum Standard by the United States, which is accompanied by a document addressing the implementation of best practices which can be accessed on the OECD website: *http://oe.cd/bepsaction14*.

Consult this publication on line at *http://dx.doi.org/10.1787/9789264282698-en*.

This work is published on the OECD iLibrary, which gathers all OECD books, periodicals and statistical databases. Visit *www.oecd-ilibrary.org* for more information.

ISBN 978-92-64-28268-1
23 2017 30 1 P